THE WONDERLAND OF LOGO DESIGN

Edited and deisgned by viction:ary

logology.2

THE WONDERLAND OF LOGO DESIGN

First published and distributed by
viction:workshop ltd.

viction:ary™

viction:workshop ltd.
Unit C, 7/F, Seabright Plaza, 9-23 Shell Street,
North Point, Hong Kong
Url: www.victionary.com   Email: we@victionary.com
www.facebook.com/victionworkshop

Edited and produced by viction:workshop ltd.

Concepts & art direction by Victor Cheung
Book design by viction:workshop ltd.

ISBN 978-988-17328-9-7
Printed and bound in China

Logology.2

THE WONDERLAND OF LOGO DESIGN

Edited and deisgned by viction:ary

viction:ary™

The space for logos has become smaller. Decades of advertising and corporate branding have left very little room for new memorable and unique marks. Cheap online services pour out endless variations of swirls and swashes and the ever-increasing power of marketing asks for safe solutions backed by consumer research rather than daring innovations.

At the same time the demand for logos is huge. You might ask why we need so many logos? Why not just set every name in a standardised font? Why bother discussing the subtle nuances and connotations of individual typefaces? In the western typographic hemisphere one explanation might lie in the constrains of the roman alphabet which is highly functional but lacks pictorial or emotional expressions. Logos make up for these shortcomings as a custom solution with bundles of carefully considered emotional messages densely packed into one plate. But these messages are already communicated on a meta-level nonetheless. As a matter of fact, we have all become masters of reading logos in the context of other logos navigating through the different layers of visual information, originally intended or acquired within a changing cultural environment.

Pictorial logos originate from trademarks. A stamp of ownership for goods in transit. Today we mostly trade in values and ideas – can those be owned? As society has changed through globalisation, so have the consumers. Their perception of a particular design have become less predictable or less likely to be guided in a preconceived direction. They want to be involved in open dialogues with brands instead of staying on the receiving end of the traditional one-way communication. More flexible logo systems are seen in recent developments that can function as platforms for free interpretation or merely decorations. Although the innocence of logo design have been lost in part in the process, the logos that we engaged with everyday have come a long way since they first appeared simply for name recognition as we look back to the earlier decades. And as consumers' expectations evolve, these factors constitutes the new challenges and even greater responsibilities with which logo designers would have to forge ahead.

FOREWORD

BY
FRÉDÉRIC
VANHORENBEKE
—
COAST
DESIGN

As graphic designers, our job is to translate complex market values with concepts that enable contextual visual identity to be at least appropriately delivered and recognisable, thinking well beyond pure graphics. The practice of design is intrinsically linked to the world around us. It is all about reflection. Understanding the disciplines that feed and influence our practice is essential: art in the broadest sense, music, politics or socio-economic environment. Understanding these entities and anticipate their evolution is the key.

A strong brand identity has a huge impact on a business, and in terms of branding, a logotype is not enough. In many cases, the process of branding can bring the client to the total redefinition of what the company is and what they do. As the number of small to medium businesses grows steadily, we teach our clients the need to create not just a logo but a brand. A strong identity is one of the key ways to help people understand their offer, and to differentiate themselves in a difficult market place where unfortunately well over half of SMEs fail in their first year.

Brand exercise shows that the relationship between time and duration has undergone a radical change directly impacting our business. It is quite possible today, in ten minutes, you can watch a video on YouTube while chatting with a customer online from another continent, touring the world's news and ordering lunch. New brands should be clear and fast reading. This is why the use of simple signs and strong forms as a reverse reflection of our global and complex world is essential. This encourages us, the creative industry, to create powerful signs of low complexity that would only take a nanosecond for anyone to identify.

Today, creating brand identities is about being simple and flexible, for all media or locations, to englobe intuitive market understanding – whether it is cultural, commercial, institutional – and reflection. In a world that is complex by nature, logos serve as the most conceptual forms of brand visualisation. A good logo communicates, and sells.

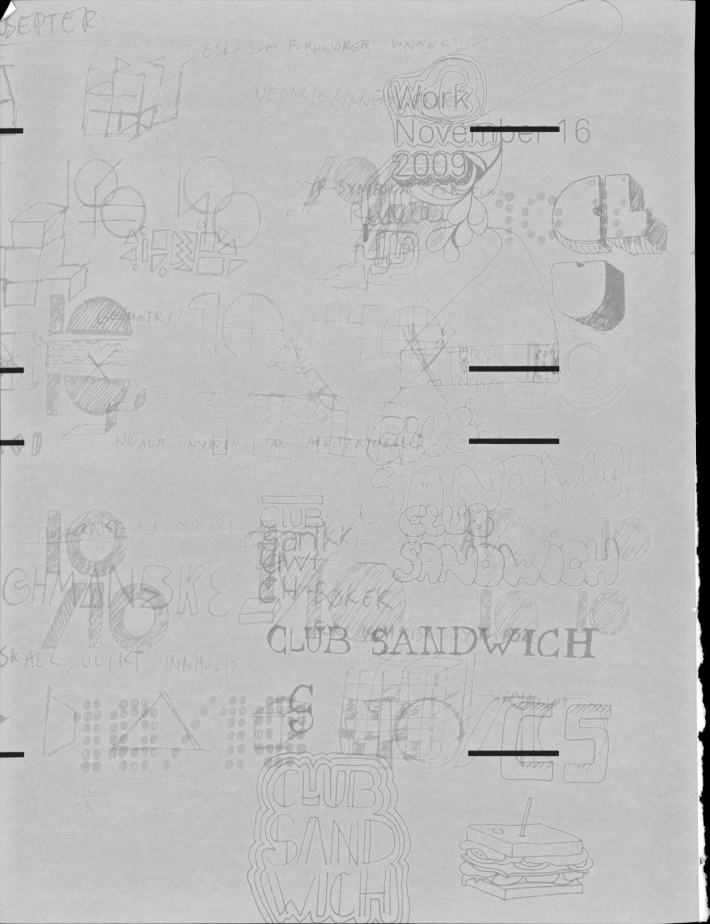

LIKE FRÉDÉRIC VANHORENBEKE SAYS, A GOOD LOGO COMMUNICATES
AND SELLS. BUT IT IS NO RANDOM RESULTS OF SOME DESIGNERS'
TECHNICAL EXCELLENCE OR ARTISTIC SENSE. A STRONG DESIGN WOULD
ALSO RELY ON GOOD COMMUNICATION AND STUDY THAT ENGAGE BOTH
THE COMMISSIONER AND DESIGNER, AND OCCASIONALLY THE INTERIOR
DESIGNERS OR ARCHITECTS, THROUGHOUT THE CREATIVE PROCESS.

HERE, WE REVISIT THE BIRTH AND GROWTH OF 13 RECENT BRANDING
AND IDENTITY PROJECTS, AND SEE HOW THE FEATURING DESIGNERS
BROKE DOWN CLIENTS' INSTRUCTIONS AND VALUES AND RESTRUCTURED
THEM WITH INSIGHTS, INSTINCTS AND VISUAL LANGUAGES THAT IMPART
FLEXIBILITY AND VISIONS AT ONCE.

PART A /
CASE STUDY

Artease Café

by Splash Productions, Singapore

A bubbly teahouse recently opened in Singapore by a team of fun and tea-loving people to introduce Taiwanese style bubble teas. To Artease, teas cheer up life as much as art does. "Without tea, life is plain arse".

THE ASSIGNMENT

The client, a local start-up selling bubble tea, had no particular direction in mind when they first approached us. They wanted a full branding exercise for their new company, including a name and logo.

However, there were some ideas from the client. They wanted something unconventional and out of the ordinary, especially when the bubble tea industry was seen quite heavily saturated at some point. They especially wanted to stay away from the traditional and very common Taiwanese-style identity that is predominant amongst the big bubble tea chains in Singapore.

THE CONCEPTION

We began by observing the three cofounders. All three were fun, bubbly and humble people, so we decided to incorporate those qualities into their branding. The concept of "three" (for the cofounders) also guided the process.

Since the client wanted something unconventional, we proposed featuring art by local artists in the brand, leading to a collaboration with a Singapore illustrator. The client also decided on the name 'Artease', which includes 'Art' and "Tease" – a name we initially proposed – to reflect the focus on art.

THE SOLUTION

The principle of the initial attempts was actually pretty similar to the final approach. We wanted to work around a shape that could be easily identified from a distance away.

The final logo features the name "Artease" against a solid circle as a tapioca "pearl", the cornerstone of bubble teas. The element of pearls and founders are also reflected in the type treatment, with three round negative spaces cut out of the word 'Artease'.

While experimenting with highlighting the word "tea" within "Artease", we discovered the hidden word "arse". We then played on this and formed the cheeky tagline – "Without tea, life is plain arse". The idea of bringing "tea" out of the word was dismissed in the final design.

Artease

THE APPLICATION

The logo is displayed on every collateral, from cups and seals to Artease's bags, stationery and storefront. As for Artease's business cards, the negative circle spaces in the logotype are actualised as die-cut holes on the card for a more tactile touch.

There are a few mascots, but the main mascot is the one with three pearls stuck together to denote the partnership of the three cofounders. The characters are as well applied on cup seals, the café's website, shop interior and other collateral.

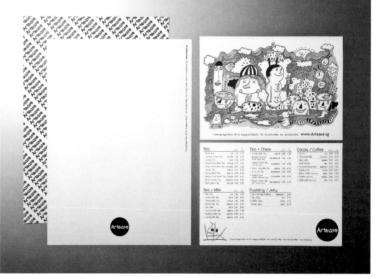

1 Tanjong Pagar Plaza #01-35 Singapore 082001 Tel: +65 6222 6966 Fax: +65 6222 6956

CASESTUDY · 02

Cardinal Café
by Hat-trick design consultants limited, London

*Housed at the entrance of Cardinal Place, a retail and office development in the heart
London's Westminster, Cardinal Café is a vast, open reception area where labour on the
entire estate could gather and chill under the sun and rains at all times.*

THE ASSIGNMENT

Cardinal Café was opened as a gathering spot for labour at the concourse of London's Cardinal Place, an architecturally pleasing commercial complex entirely enfolded in glass curtain walls.

The brief of this identity project was to create a name and branding for the café, including signage, wall graphics, crockery and other collateral.

"USING A CHARACTER MEANT THAT VIBRANCY AND ACTIVITY WAS CREATED IN THE CAFE AREA, KEEPING IT DISTINCT FROM THE CORPORATE RECEPTION AREA."

THE CONCEPTION

We wanted a jolly, upbeat character that would keep the brand alive and interesting, so we started doodling on napkins until we came to using the Cardinal bird which shares its name with the location. The bird was named for its resemblance to a Catholic cardinal's red robe and cap.

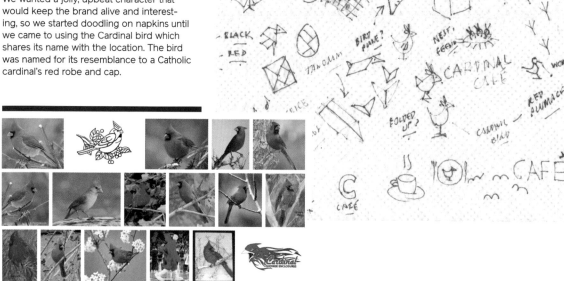

THE SOLUTION

The café borrows the name of the bird and, thus, Cardinal Café. We designed the character as a tangram so that we could have lots of small variations. Having a changing and evolving mark helps to keep the brand alive and interesting.

CARDINAL
CAFÉ

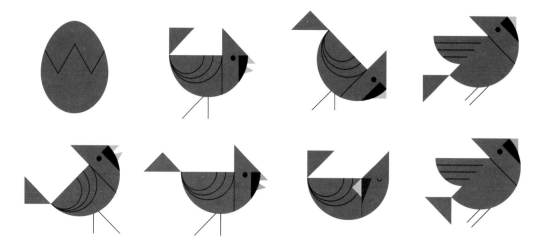

Characters would give the café area a sense of vibrancy and activity. We are not interested in simply putting the same logo on everything like a corporate wallpaper. Graphics are applied using vinyl, which can be easily updated, allowing the birds to 'move' around the area over time.

We think the tip box was a good extension of the overall idea. The cups were originally used in the café but since they kept getting stolen, they are now for sale.

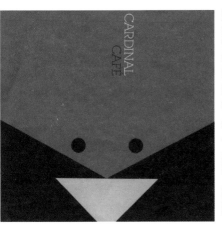

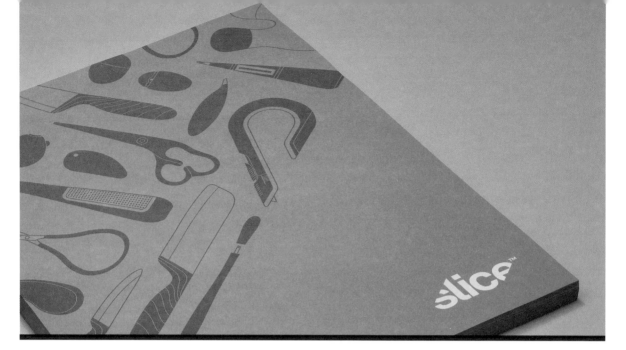

Slice

by Manual, San Francisco

Founded by TJ Scimone in 2008, Slice works with world-renowned designers to design and manufacture innovative cutting tools for homes and offices. Most of its products are a celebration of vibrant colour, bold design and extraordinary function.

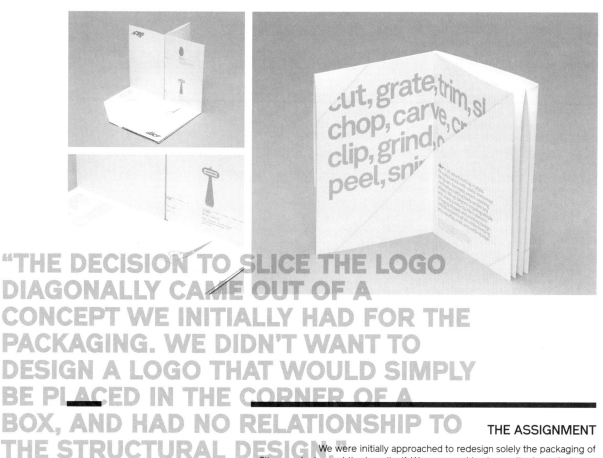

"THE DECISION TO SLICE THE LOGO DIAGONALLY CAME OUT OF A CONCEPT WE INITIALLY HAD FOR THE PACKAGING. WE DIDN'T WANT TO DESIGN A LOGO THAT WOULD SIMPLY BE PLACED IN THE CORNER OF A BOX, AND HAD NO RELATIONSHIP TO THE STRUCTURAL DESIGN."

THE ASSIGNMENT

We were initially approached to redesign solely the packaging of Slice products - not the logo itself. We proposed to change the logo design as we felt there was an opportunity to manifest the graphic identity on the packaging in a more interesting and iconic manner than we could with their old logo. We had to sell the idea by showing the clients the potential since they had not originally tasked us with a logo redesign.

THE CONCEPTION

The original logo was an orange wordmark, spelling the word 'Slice' in Helvetica Bold, with its bottom snipped off horizontally.

We thought the cut was a perfectly apt element but a shift could make it a much dynamic logotype and interesting on the packaging.

THE SOLUTION

The result itself is very straightforward. It did not go through many rounds of development as we were confident about the solution.

We finally landed upon Akkurat Bold, which seems to carry a little more character than Helvetica with a serif "l" as a nice little addition to the otherwise angular wordmark.

The final result sparked a whole graphic language around the sliced angles on both ends. The client immediately saw the value in how the angles could be exploited in the packaging materials and structures that let the packaging speak the concept.

We had proposed to adopt a warm red colour (P032) but the client was not convinced, for the brand equity and recognition that have already been established in the original orange colour, so the idea was dropped.

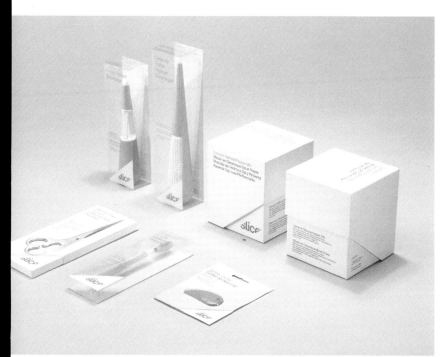

THE APPLICATION

We felt the original packaging was a little too garish and bright, so we adopted a much minimal approach, with less orange against abundant white to accent the product. The slash element and the minimal principle are visible throughout Slice's corporate designs.

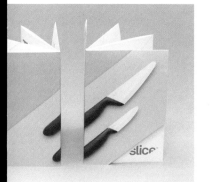

The People's Supermarket

by Unreal, London

A sustainable food cooperative set up by British chef Arthur Potts-Dawson. The supermarket and restaurant is entirely staffed by local residents and offers locally grown produce and menus at fair prices.

"KEEPING THE MESSAGE SIMPLE IS FUNDAMENTAL TO ANY BRAND AND IDENTITY... IT SHOULD BE STRIPPED BACK AS FAR AS POSSIBLE AND THEN LOVINGLY CRAFTED."

THE ASSIGNMENT

We were tasked with creating the brand and identity for the supermarket to reflect its core values of communal, affordable and democratic without appearing too virtuous or elitist.

The supermarket had also asked for a sub-brand identity for its own kitchen, The People's Kitchen, where Arthur Potts-Dawson would cook with ingredients available from the supermarket.

The full identity programme covered logo, stationery suite, advertising, packaging and guidelines.

THE CONCEPTION

In the search and development of branding ideas, we stumbled upon the euro-slot, the little punch hole that goes unnoticed at the top of packaged products despite being synonymous with retail around the world. We felt the punch shape would be easy to recognise, basic, honest and symbolic of utilitarian. It represents a wholesome, independent, classic shopping experience as one of the cooperative's intent.

THE SOLUTION

Since much of the packaging and print materials would have to be produced in-store, designs will have to be simple to implement.

The final identity is a simple, clever and cost-effective branding device based on the classic euro-slot that can be consistently applied on anything from letterheads to in-store packaging. The hole punch can be purchased from eBay for £12.50.

THE PEOPLE'S SUPERMARKET

For the people, by the people

LAMB'S CONDUIT ST. LONDON

THE APPLICATION

The completed project is friendly in its look and utilitarian in approach. The logo and euro-slot itself has evolved to form everything from labels for packaging to handles of the market's shopping bags and tabs on its ads.

The final branding scheme was rolled out across stationery, in-store signage, advertising, own-brand packaging, shop window decals and brand guidelines in its theme colour, yellow and black. Much of the printing was done in-house at Unreal on GF Smith Colorplan Pristine White.

OKINAHA

by Coast Design, Brussels

Founded by two pharmacists, Okinaha is set to be Europe's first concept store on health and anti-aging. The store features a combination of functional zones for shopping, spa experience and learning as a holistic approach to health and well-being.

"STANDING AGAINST COMPETITORS IS NOT ALWAYS THE BEST SOLUTIONS FOR BRANDS. BRANDS HAVE TO ACT ACCORDINGLY TO SOME KIND OF INCONSCIOUS REFERENCES THEIR CUSTOMERS HAVE."

THE ASSIGNMENT

Representing new visions of health and wellness, Okinaha founded its concepts on the cultural features of Okinawa, one of Japan's southern prefectures, where inhabitants generally enjoy longer lives. The store offers a range of products, including cosmetics and supplements containing ingredients obtainable from the island. The project was a branding exercise for the new concept store.

THE CONCEPTION

Our first step for creating this new brand was to character its emphases on longevity and purity with a strong influence of Okinawa. We wanted the shop to be precise and modern, a mix between a luxury shop and a spa house.

Okinawa.com was not an available domain name at that point. The name 'Okinaha' is an infusion of 'Okinawa' and 'Naha', the prefecture's main city.

OKINAHA

OKI_NAHA

OKINAHA

OKINAHA

OKI_NAHA

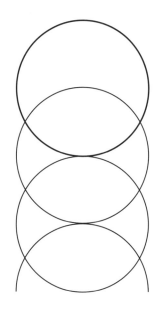

ITC avant garde extra light

abcdefghijklmn
opqrstuvwxyz
ABCDEFGHIJKLMN
OPQRSTUVWXYZ
0123456789
(*/=°!?&@#)-%*$£

THE SOLUTION

The idea of projecting oriental simplicity in Okinaha was there from the start. Brand elements, e.g. the "rising sun" logotype, an "anti-aging secrets" brochure and the store interior were oriented to ensure co-branding associations and push Okinaha into the community of brands of which it needs to be a part.

ITC avant garde book

abcdefghijklmn
opqrstuvwxyz
ABCDEFGHIJKLMN
OPQRSTUVWXYZ
0123456789
(*/=°!?&@#)-%*$£

OKINAHA

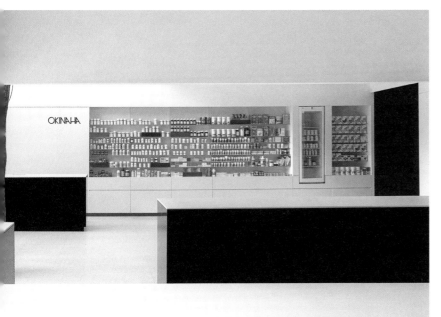

THE APPLICATION

Brands have to act accordingly to some kind of unconscious references their customers have. In that case, for Okinaha's first premium concept store, our design, from the principles to its implement, would somehow have to allude to the idea of well-being that have been built up by its like-brands.

All of our creative output were inspired by luxurious purity and oriental simplicity, aiming for an environment where customer can relax while shopping for health. Real tree strucks were added to create an indoor forest to link longevity with nature in the shop.

Brand elements are inscribed on everything from the store's interior to its narrative elements, such as bags and stationery items, to bring continuity. The logo featuring a rising sun was incrusted beside the cashier counter to accentuate the theme.

Micheline Fine Prints

by Anagrama, San Pedro Garza García

Since the mid-1970s, Micheline has been making a success in producing quality design and high-end printing under the same roof, chiefly for social events. The print house has relied much of its business on its loyal customers until the recent shift in ownership.

"IT IS ALWAYS GOOD TO AVOID LITERALLY REPRESENTING THE COMPANY'S SERVICE. THAT IS WHY THE APPLE ICON WORKS SO WELL..., IT SAYS HOW THE COMPANY AND ITS VALUES ARE DIAMETRICALLY DIFFERENT FROM ITS COMPETITORS."

THE ASSIGNMENT

Micheline's business has been successful for many years because of its social connections, but as their loyal costumers grow old and due to a change in ownership, the new owners felt a significant decrease in their magnetism and, thus, an urge to renew their brand to appeal to a younger crowd.

For that, they wanted their brand and store to express a sense of uniqueness, elegance, and above all, modernity.

THE CONCEPTION

Our job was to renovate a historical space that had paid no attention to design for the last 30 years. We needed to take away its "local business" aesthetics and create a whole new experience for printing and design.

Our detonators for branding are mostly external due to more sophisticated competitors worldwide. By enhancing the elegance of the company's stationery design and the staff's clothing etc., we wanted to turn Micheline into a premium print shop for young adults through a stimulating experience.

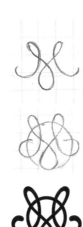
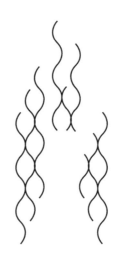

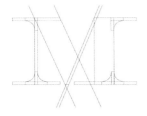
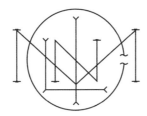

THE SOLUTION

Having gone through three different internal identity proposals, we created a clean black and white identity with some colour accents and finishes that will age with style, as one of our primary objectives. We also designed a monogram that would be easily produced into stickers and adhesive tapes to apply on their print products as printshop's signature.

As for the interiors, with the help of collaborators such as German Dehesa and Roberto Treviño, we constructed a seventies print shop environment with its vanguardist spirit accentuated by a few contemporary elements such as the lighting.

A neutral tone was used to draw attention to the racks and the colourful printing catalogues, so as to highlight the brand's presence.

An array of geometric and asymmetric patterns on the backdrop was also adopted along the identity to create a visually interesting system around contrast and nostalgic settings.

THE APPLICATION

It is the variety and eclectic style that makes the brand pops out. A diversity of patterns was developed but united by its black-and-white theme colour for its packaging, opening invitation and in-store decoration etc., against its colourful prints.

The idea was to let Micheline's name invade its shop and customers' minds in multiple ways and appearances, rather than just in the body of a logo design.

MIDI
by Coast Design, Brussels

Offering a fresh combination of honest canteen food in the daytime at K-nal, Brussels, midi segues into a vivid party space when the sun goes down. The eatery was originally named "Club Sandwich".

"IDENTITY IS A QUESTION
OF BRANDING, AND BRANDING IS A
QUESTION OF AUDIENCE. BUILDING
A STRONG BRAND IS ABOUT
UNDERSTANDING THE WAYS OF
NEW CONSUMERISM."

THE ASSIGNMENT

We were assigned to create a logotype and a global imagery for a new restaurant housed in a very industrial two-storey building, overlooking the port and
the canal of Brussels. The client was initially named "Club Sandwich" to highlight
its sandwich menu.

THE CONCEPTION

The original club sandwich identity was much based on the sense of a club experience, with visuals based on illustrations. We do like brands to have a strong immediate approach, like Apple or Playmobil, with a strong statement about who they are and what they do.

'MIDI' was indeed more radical and direct. After a tour of questioning, the name was chosen for its meaning of 'noon' in French, its length and capacity to imply broader food suggestions. We wanted a name that could strike attention, and when people think of lunch (at noon), they would go to MIDI. The word also offers a number of possible extensions, such as 'soir', French for 'evening', if the client wishes to expand its business.

Our client showed us the kind of furniture he was going for, which were vintage school (or university) tables and chairs in colours of red, yellow and blue. Other influences were the industrial look of the building and the simplicity of the menu and food proposed.

THE SOLUTION

We felt the graphics would have to be simple and bold. We decided to take their furniture as a starting point for creation and the result is an identity based on the furniture colours centered around a strong-yet-playful logotype.

For a lunch place where people come to relax between meetings and a day of work, Lineto's KADA font was exactly what we desired. It is bold and fun, with the contrasting colours incorporated into individual strokes.

A set of pictograms were also developed along the mark to create a visual playground for the mid-day break!

THE APPLICATION

We wanted to build brand appearance in many situations. We wanted to have this simple approach for MIDI's branding like it was in the 1960s and 1970s – duplicate the logotype and let it tell the brand.

The logotype is very versatile in application. By switching the colours of the alternative strokes, the logo makes a vibrant impression for anyone who is holding MIDI's menu, food tray, number box, and most importantly its food and beverages in hand. Where the construction of brand images depends on its audience and the message you want to relate, here the subject is about simplicity and "It's only food. Let's play".

CASESTUDY · 08

10/10 Arper Stylecraft Launch
by THERE, Surry Hills (NSW)

A Stylecraft road show was launched to celebrate the introduction of ten product ranges from Arper, and ten years of successful partnership with the Italian furniture manufacturer. The one-off celebration was on tour throughout Australia for a month.

"THERE IS NO REAL DIFFERENCE DESIGNING FOR AN EVENT OR A BUSINESS. THE PROJECT OBJECTIVES, BRIEFING AND COMMUNICATION IMPERATIVES OFTEN STEER AND INFORM THE CREATIVE OUTCOME."

THE ASSIGNMENT

To celebrate the launching of ten new products from Italian furniture supplier Arper and the tenth year of being Arper's exclusive distributor in Australia, Stylecraft planned a series of seminal showcase events at each of their showrooms across the cities of Melbourne, Sydney, Brisbane and Adelaide.

The commission here was to create a comprehensive and engaging experience to promote the events.

THE CONCEPTION

The client would be expecting professionals, such as architects, interior designers, specifiers of furniture at the event, so the approach would have to be understated, elegant, sophisticated and contemporary.

10/10 was to be the biggest product launch for Stylecraft and a comprehensive and engaging customer experience was required to promote and accompany the event. We took the conjunction of launching of ten new products and the ten years of partnership between Stylecraft and Arper, thus '10/10'.

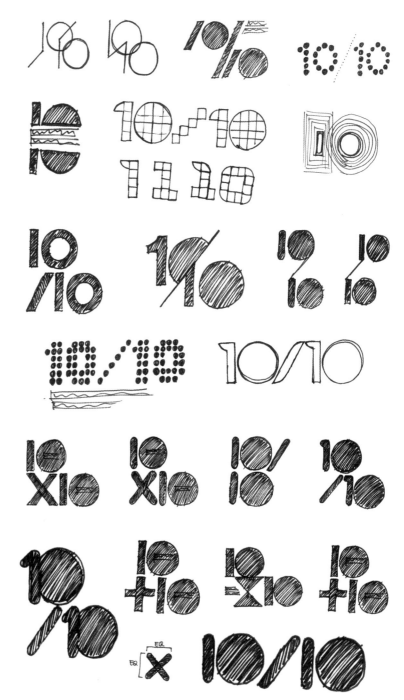

STYLECRAFT & ARPER
10 RANGES CELEBRATING
10 YEARS TOGETHER

THE SOLUTION

Taking cues from our recent Stylecraft rebranding exercise (see casestudy 09), we developed a range of playful and sophisticated identity solutions.

The 10/10 event logo conveyed a clean and slick aesthetic, yet boasting playful and fun appeal, targeted at the specifier market, architects and interior designers.

We expanded the secondary palette of magenta to fit the Stylecraft brand. The multiple colours of the events were also reflective of Arper's distinctive products, creating a fun and playful colour system to bring the event collateral to life.

THE APPLICATION

From initial concept through to installation, every stage was well-planned and executed. The Stylecraft and Arper logos were seen throughout the event and on most applications, from external signage and interior display to banners, posters, invitations, badges and DVD packs, as a low emphasis for the hosts at the showroom.

The identity and playful circular design language informed all promotional collateral and POS display items, with client's product ranges perfectly complemented by colours, tone and imagery, to initiate conversations amongst the audience and organisers' potential clients.

The showroom space was broken up and divided by various suspended acrylic discs, allowing guests to navigate themselves around, thus making it an engaging and experiential event. The circular discs were often swivelling and rotating, encouraging visitors to interact with them.

GINGER

DESIGNED BY
JEAN-MARIE MASSAUD

A new collection of tables suitable for hospitality environments.

Featuring a polypropylene table top and with the base finished to polished or powdercoated aluminium, the Ginger table is suitable for outdoor use.

Ginger is available in three heights for added versatility.

NORMA

D BY
ALTHERR MOLINA

s suitability for hospitality
Arper are now offering the
chair in a stackable model.

holstery now offered as a
dition to leather, the Norma
ease in contemporary
s.

w lounge and barstool
collection.

NUUR

DESIGNED BY
SIMON PENGE

A clean and stylish des
is the hallmark of the ne

The square or rectangu
table collection is availa
or veneer tops with alur
to a polished or powder

The Nuur table won the
iF Product Design Awar

Stylecraft Rebranding

by THERE, Surry Hills (NSW)

A contemporary furniture retailer for corporate, government, hospitality, public and residential spaces around Australia and Asia. Their offerings are a collection of exclusive European and Australian furniture and lighting brands, including Arper, Catifa and Tacchini.

"IDENTITY IS... HOW
A (NAME) COMES TO LIFE
AS A LIVING, BREATHING BRAND.
THE SUCCESS OF STYLECRAFT'S
BRAND IS THAT, EVEN IF
YOU TOOK THE LOGO
AWAY, CUSTOMER WOULD
STILL RECOGNISE IT AS
STYLECRAFT. THAT IS THE POWER
OF STRONG BRANDING."

THE ASSIGNMENT

When Stylecraft came to THERE, they were happy with their existing logo, however, it lacked strong supporting graphic language and was becoming a little 'stale'. THERE was invited to 'bring the brand to life' and inject a more playful, dynamic and aesthetically beautiful approach that would reflect the fun, bubbly and design passionate team more genuinely.

THE CONCEPTION

The Stylecraft logo was originally a plain understated mark that lacks a sense of fun and playfulness, so we started by taking the primary 'circular' device and playfully developed a range of geometric icons where retro chic meets the avant-garde.

We assessed Stylecraft's existing colour palette, and felt that both grey and the strong vibrant magenta would look appealing to the architects and achieve cut-through in the market places. The colours would also reflect the fun nature and personality of Stylecraft's staff.

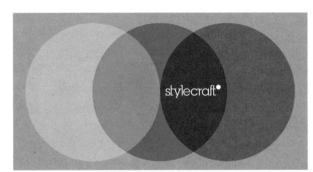

Original design by Alphabet Studio

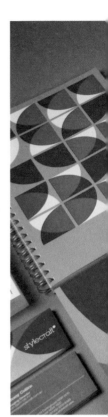

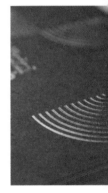

THE SOLUTION

Working together our team developed the Stylecraft logo from a plain understated mark that the Stylecraft personnel was so well known for.

We took the circles and dots from the existing logo and had it evolved, multiplied, dissected, rotated to achieve a visual library of graphic languages that can be mixed and interchanged, to keep the brand always interesting and fresh. We expanded on the secondary palette of colours ranging from neon magenta through to dark maroon, and a typographic hierarchy, with Lublin Graph as the primary display font and contemporary classic Helvetica Neue for the everyday secondary body copy font.

THE APPLICATION

The execution of the applications was a more effective, bold and daring approach. We believe the sign of a successful brand is to have the brand easily recognised within the industry, without the need to see the logo itself.

Through careful 'crafting', the new branding system effectively communicates the Stylecraft's undeniable curation 'style', making Stylecraft a brand truth.

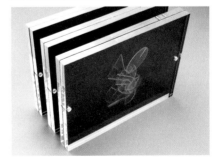

Deichmanske Library

by Mikael Fløysand, Oslo

The new library was looking to become one of the most modern and functional libraries in Europe. The public body is set to be as both a traditional library and modern cultural institution in Bjørvika, Oslo. Deichmanske Library was a hypothetical client in this project.

"BRANDING IS JUST AS IMPORTANT FOR NON-PROFIT ORGANISATIONS… EVEN IF THE LIBRARY IS NOT SUPPOSED TO MAKE MONEY, THEY STILL NEED VISITORS, AND THE PUBLIC NEEDS TO BE AWARE THAT THEY EXIST AND WHAT THEY CAN OFFER."

THE ASSIGNMENT

The project was for my second year final exam at Westerdals School of Communication. Here, the new Deichmanske Library saw itself to be much more than a library as it would accommodate facilities such as theatre space for concerts, a café or bar, lecture halls and debate forums, embracing old library traditions and new-age digital media in one body. The institution was scheduled to be built in Bjørvika, Oslo, over the next years. It needed an identity that could reflect the library as a 21st century institution.

THE CONCEPTION

As I started out researching existing library identities, I quickly found out that the majority is rather a traditional historical representation of the public bodies. To highlight the library's multifunctionality and let it stand out as a modern institution, I expressly shunned the word "Library" in its name, so as to focus on "the institution" as a whole and not just the library part. But the name Deichmanske is quite well known in Oslo as several libraries were already carrying the name.

Although the library was still in construction, both official architectural drawings and documents about how the new library was supposed to function were all available to hand. I assumed everyone in the city to be its audience, but the identity would have to be attractive for people who were not aware of the institution or the services it offered.

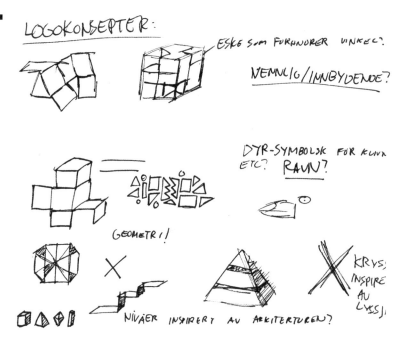

LOGOKONSEPTER:

ESKE SOM FORANDRER VINKEL?

VENNLIG / INNBYDENDE?

GEOMETRI!

DYR-SYMBOLSK FOR KUNN ETC? RAVN?

KRYS; INSPIRE AV LYSS;

NIVÅER INSPIRERT AV ARKITEKTUREN?

DEICHMANSKE BIBLIOTEK

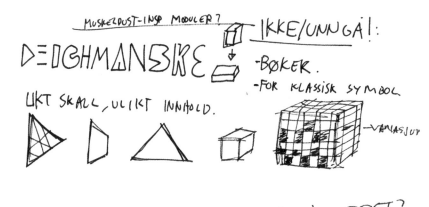

MUSKEDUST-INSP MODULER?

DEICHMANSKE

IKKE/UNNGÅ!:
-BØKER.
-FOR KLASSISK SYMBOL

LIKT SKALL, ULIKT INNHOLD.

-VANNASJON

PIKTOGRAMMER RELEVANTE ISTEDET?

BOK

LYSPÆRE

CD

UGLE

DVD

MAGASIN!

KONSERT

*DEICHMANSKE   *DEICHMANSKE   *DEICHMANSKE

*DEICHMANSKE   *DEICHMANSKE   *DEICHMANSKE

THE SOLUTION

The final solution was a family of seven logos of which the geometric construction would constantly evolve to denote the many facets of the library, just as the library itself was supposed. The logos were a main element of the identity package.

And as I wanted the design to look modern but yet convey a traditional atmosphere, a retro mood is partly intended. Akkurat Pro, heavily influenced by Helvetica but with an updated look, was chosen to create a simple typographic system to supplement the logos.

I also used yellowed paper stock to accentuate the organisation's modernity while giving it a homely feel. Few organisations think of paper as a way to stand out, but it is a nice thing to use as a design element in itself.

*DEICHMANSKE

*DEICHMANSKE   *DEICHMANSKE   *DEICHMANSKE

*DEICHMANSKE   *DEICHMANSKE   *DEICHMANSKE   *DEICHMANSKE

THE APPLICATION

The logos have become the key element of the entire identity system, with it becoming the body of the library's corporate business cards, as logos, illustrations and patterns – basis of all corporate communication matter that includes two sets of monocolour posters as well as editorial design.

The library will also publish a collection of stylish products and stationery like notepads, bookmarks and totebags etc, which carries the two-colour marks.

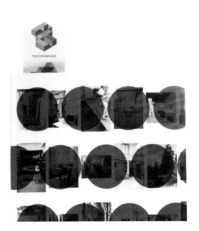

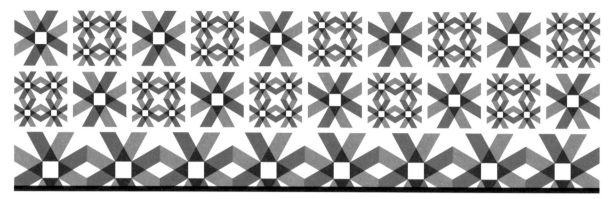

ZURICH 2012

by George Strouzas, Athens

Held every four years by different host cities, the Olympic Games place their values on excellence, respect and friendship. The international event's objective is to build a better world where equality exists among sexes, races and people with different abilities.

"A LOGO DESIGNED FOR SUCH EVENT HAS MORE DON'TS THAN DOS. I TRIED TO SHOW UNITY OF THE PEOPLE ON THE LOGO AND AVOID FORMS THAT WOULD REMIND OF ANY RELIGION OR COLOUR DISCRETION."

THE ASSIGNMENT

Zurich 2012 was a self-initiated identity project, with a goal to promote the Games to occur in Zurich, the largest city of Switzerland, in 2012.

For such an international event, the identity shall allow the city to declare herself in a universal way. As to address people of different background and ages, it should be a classic trademark based on neutrality and dynamics while indicating equality and the unity of people from around the world.

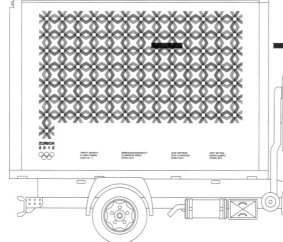

THE CONCEPTION

During my research on Switzerland, I learned about the country's long tradition of graphic design based around flat visuals and vacant spaces laid out on grid systems besides typography, if we look back to the influential decades when International Typographic Style was introduced. That was where I started designing with form as the basis.

It also came to my knowledge that the Swiss speaks three languages, which took me to impart the element of "parts" of the world in the design, besides neutrality, clarity, strength and finally unity.

Helvetica Black

**ABCDEFGHI
JKLMNOPQR
STUVWXYZ
0123456789**

THE SOLUTION

The final Zurich 2012 logo shows four people as four pairs of legs, all from a different direction – North, South, West, East – and unified in an abstracted way. In the middle where the legs came together and overlapped, it symbolises unity and reconciliation, a place common to all.

The name of the city was written in Helvetica a completely neutral typeface originated from Switzerland. Sizes and kerning of the text component were customised for better readability and easy recognition.

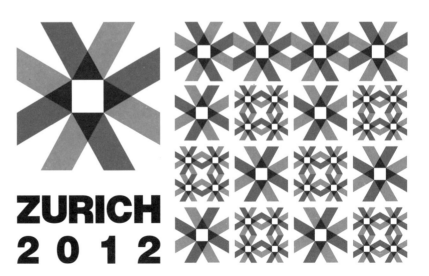

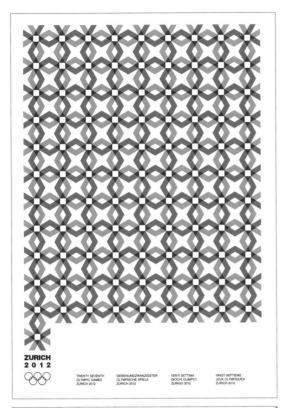

THE APPLICATION

The logo was used in all applications as a unit. It was also multiplied to form a pattern, showing once again the universality of the Olympic Games.

The products and applications to be produced as souvenirs, staff's uniform or marketing collateral during the Games include posters, T-shirts and badges. Special attention was particularly given to posters and banners design with regard to the rules that have been there since the 1950s. It was hard to be expressive when the rules state that the posters would have to be so simple yet innovative that anyone in the city would be stimulated and find it easy to read, understand and remember. But, to me, the result was really legible, and that made the point!

CIRCUS
by Mind Design, London

The new West End cocktail bar and London cabaret restaurant combination is set in vibrant Covent Garden, the heart of theatre-land. The London performance restaurant boasts a stylish surrealist interior designed by British designer Tom Dixon.

Interior design: Design Research Studio
Photography: Mark Whitfield

"WE ENJOY WORKING WITH FLEXIBLE LOGO SYSTEMS AS THEY OFTEN MAKE THE OVERALL IDENTITY MORE RICH AND INTERESTING. HOWEVER, THERE SHOULD ALWAYS BE A PRACTICAL OR CONCEPTUAL REASON FOR USING SEVERAL LOGO VARIATIONS."

THE ASSIGNMENT

Circus is a new restaurant and bar in West End of London. It features live performances with a burlesque character, often acrobatic and sometimes just pure fun. Guests would often be surprised when the dining table in the centre suddenly becomes the stage.

The brief was to design an identity that relates to the interior and various aspects that create the overall mood of the place.

THE CONCEPTION

Influences came from a range of subjects spanning Surrealism, Art Deco, Alice in Wonderland, animals, so as the building where Circus is housed, leading up to the large table that doubles as a stage. Rumour has it the construction had been used to accommodate elephants for performances in the West End back in the Victorian times, which apparently matches the restaurant's circus theme.

THE SOLUTION

Since the club's interior features many mirrored surfaces, the logo design was based on the structure of a kaleidoscope. While the basic construction of the logo remains the same, the inside varies with applications, e.g. materialised in layers and illuminated at the entrance and cut out from the packaging box.

For the type, we wanted to use an Art Deco font since Revue theatres were popular during that period. The font we finally adopted has a triangle instead of a horizontal bar in the upper case 'A' which relates to the logo.

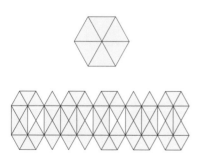

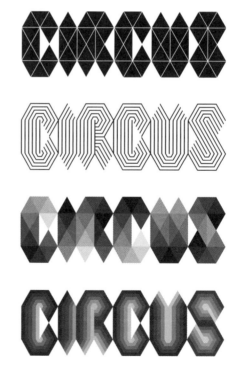

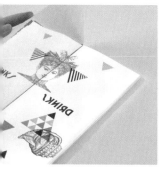

Photography: Mark Whitfield

THE APPLICATION

As the logos carry a unique context in each application, from signage systems to items as small as cloakroom tabs, the variety fuels the burlesque atmosphere within the restaurant.

Most interestingly and technically challenging was the design of the huge 'Circus' sign set into a mirrored wall at the entrance area. We spent a long time building dummies and testing ways of illuminating the sign with colourful LEDs, but still it was hard to predict how the final installation would look in the actual space. But we think it turned out really well. The logo was built into sandwiched layers of semi transparent acrylic with a certain depth.

While animals obviously relate to the circus theme, they also play an important role in Surrealism. So a set of table mats were designed, so guests can create their own little freakshow by combining different heads and bodies when sitting at the bar.

RAVENSBOURNE

by johnson banks, London

Formerly Ravensbourne College of Design and Communication, Ravensbourne is a higher education sector college specialising in design and broadcasting. It was relocated to its current address in 2009 when they approach johnson banks for an identity update.

THE ASSIGNMENT

Ravensbourne was about to be moved from its previous Chislehurst home to a new landmark building next to the 02/Dome in Greenwich.

We were asked to help create a new verbal and visual identity that would reflect the huge change in emphasis that the new building has brought – a digital future and innovation.

"A BRAND CAN BE VISUAL AND VERBAL IT CAN PERMEATE THROUGH EVERYTHING FROM CORPORATE STRATEGY TO VALUES, DESIGN, IMPLEMENTATION & COMMUNICATIONS. LOGOS FUNCTION AS AN ICEBERG AND EVERYTHING STEMS FROM IT."

THE CONCEPTION

The building's design is dominated by tens of thousands of anodised aluminium tiles, designed by mathematical physicist Sir Roger Penrose, punctuated by circular glass panes.

We saw the beauty of the tessellation pattern as it seemed to vary continuously with just a few basic shapes. We decided that this visual signature should be included in the visual identity as the apt educational analogy to indicate potential and infinity possibilities.

THE SOLUTION

Once we realised that the building was covered in 30,000 tiles, in quite an aperiodic style, we took three tiles as the key element, and threw each of them at a different angle with fragments of the name integrated into it. We have also made it integral to the scheme with multiple combinations of the logo itself.

In total there were six different combinations. We have chosen the versions where the different perspectives would generate illusions of motion, either about to resolve, or to spin again. The result was a series of symbols that never seemed to 'rest' – always moving, always searching, always adapting – not like 'stills' of an animation.

THE APPLICATION

A key part of the scheme is a set of photograph shoots of students from Ravensbourne, retouched to incorporate the pattern. These images are displayed across the scheme, which includes stationery, a biased-edge prospectus and the proposed approach to the web. The geometric elements were also adopted as 3D 'wraps' of the building across shapes and objects for future applications as well as signage and wayfinding within the building.

Jill Hogan
**Head of Marketing
and Communications**

Ravensbourne
6 Penrose Way
London
SE10 0EW

T   +44 (0)20 3040 3500
M   +44 (0)7912 999 312
E   j.hogan@rave.ac.uk

www.rave.ac.uk

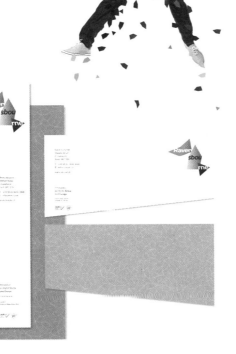

Prospectus
2011–2012

Innovation
in Digital Media
and Design

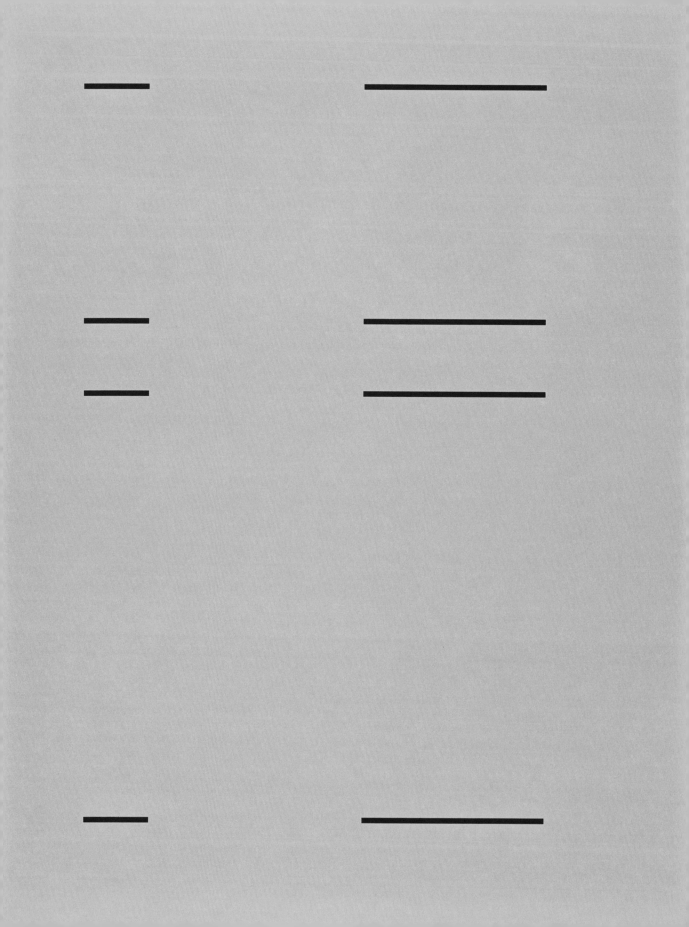

FIRST EMERGED AS PICTORIAL NAMES TO DIFFERENTIATE PRODUCERS IN
THE MARKET, LOGOS TODAY SPEAK A MUCH SOPHISTICATE LANGUAGE
THAT CATERS FOR THE WORLD. WHETHER THEY DRAW ON SYMBOLISM
TO TRANSMIT MEANINGS OR LETTERFORMS AND ALPHABETS TO IMPART
PROMISES, 'SIMPLE' REMAINS THE KEY TO GET A LARGER CROWD INVOLVED.

MAPPED OUT IN GALLERY IS A LIST OF GRAPHIC ICONS AND LOGOTYPES
THAT HAVE RECENTLY COME TO PREVAIL THE SCENE AND CATCH
IMAGINATION AROUND THE INTERNET AND THE MATERIAL WORLD.
RESPECTIVE CATEGORIES AND SUBCATEGORIES ARE INDICATED IN THE
HEADER SPACE OF EACH PAGE, WITH DESIGN CREDITS UNDERNEATH THE
SHOWCASE.

PART B /
GALLERY

- 1 -

- 2 -

- 3 -

- 4 -

- 5 -

- 6 -

- 7 -

- 8 -

1. Give Up Art, Matt Jenkins / 2. Studio Lin / 3, 7, 8. EMPK ATELIER / A / 4. Mirko Ilic Corp. / 5. Deuce Design / 6. Lundgren+Lindqvist

- 1 -

- 2 -

- 3 -

- 4 -

- 5 -

- 6 -

- 7 -

- 8 -

1. The KDU / 2. HelloMe™ / 3. Design Ranch / 4. Creuna / 5. Melvin Galapon, Meirion Pritchard / 6. cypher13 / 7. Face. / 8. Fontan 2

- 1 -

- 2 -

- 3 -

- 4 -

- 5 -

- 6 -

- 7 -

- 8 -

- 9 -

1. DixonBaxi / 2. The Made Shop / 3. Ah&Oh Studio / 4. Give Up Art / 5. Mikey Burton / 6. Robin Ramsell / 7. Ian Lynam Design / 8. NNSS / 9. cypher13

- 1 -

- 2 -

- 3 -

- 4 -

- 5 -

- 6 -

- 7 -

- 8 -

- 9 -

1. Renato Forster / 2. Chris Wharton / 3. Taste Inc. / 4. Studio Brito78 / 5. Made Agency / 6. gardens&co. / 7. FEED / 8, 9. Jee-eun Lee, Yona Lee

- 1 -

- 2 -

- 3 -

- 4 -

- 5 -

- 6 -

- 7 -

- 8 -

1. gardens&co. / 2. Stylo Design / 3. inly products / 4. Jamfactory / 5, 7. Celeste Prevost / 6. cypher13 / 8. Barbara Muriungi

- 1 -

Full Stop.

- 2 -

- 3 -

PITA & PAUL

- 4 -

- 5 -

- 6 -

- 7 -

- 8 -

B·007

1. Celeste Prevost / 2. G-MAN / 3, 5. cypher13 / 4. Nikolaus Schmidt Design / 6. Dirty Little Secret / 7. Glitz Design / 8. 38one, LLC

- 1 -

- 2 -

- 3 -

- 4 -

- 5 -

- 6 -

- 7 -

- 8 -

- 9 -

1. cypher13 / 2. Barbara Muriungi / 3. Coast Design / 4. Face. / 5. ALVA® / 6. Elena Dvoretskaya Mayagrafik / 7. Mash Creative / 8. Tönky /
9. + WONKSITE STUDIO +

- 1 -

- 2 -

- 3 -

- 4 -

- 5 -

- 6 -

- 7 -

- 8 -

- 9 -

1. HelloMe™ / 2. Parent / 3. viction:workshop ltd. / 4. Jonas Halfter / 5. Horacio Lorente / 6. Alex Cornell / 7. Cardon Webb / 8. THERE / 9. visualism | design & direction

- 1 -

- 2 -

- 3 -

- 4 -

- 5 -

- 6 -

- 7 -

- 8 -

1. Rubber Design / 2. Greg Christman / 3. Draplin Design Co. / 4. Ideas You Forgot / 5. Everything / 6. Lundgren+Lindqvist / 7. HelloMe™ /
8. ICG (Intereurope Communications Group)

- 1 -

- 2 -

- 3 -

- 4 -

- 5 -

- 6 -

- 7 -

- 8 -

- 9 -

B-011

1, 5. cypher13 / 2. Wink, Incorporated / 3. JJAAKK / 4. Glasfurd & Walker Design / 6. Larimie Garcia / 7. Dalston Creative / 8. Stylo Design / 9. Mikey Burton

GRAPHIC ICON	GEOMETRY	ANIMATE	CIRCLE : MULTICOLOUR	POLYGON
LOGOTYPE	ABSTRACT	LIFESTYLE	QUADRILATERAL	
	EMBLEM	VEGETATION	TRIANGLE	

- 1 -

- 2 -

- 3 -

- 4 -

- 5 -

- 6 -

- 7 -

- 8 -

- 9 -

1. think simple act simple. / 2. ICE CREAM FOR FREE™ / 3. Studio Brave / 4. Stoëmp Studio / 5. Kern02 graphic design / 6. AKACORLEONE /
7. Mihail Mihaylov / 8. Paperjam Design Ltd. / 9. Mikey Burton

- 1 -

- 2 -

- 3 -

- 4 -

B·013

GRAPHIC ICON	GEOMETRY	ANIMATE	CIRCLE : DETAILED	POLYGON
LOGOTYPE	ABSTRACT	LIFESTYLE	QUADRILATERAL	
	EMBLEM	VEGETATION	TRIANGLE	

- 1 -

- 2 -

- 3 -

- 4 -

1. Greg Christman / 2. Rina Miele / 3. Hiekka Graphics / 4. André Beato

- 1 -

- 2 -

- 3 -

- 4 -

- 5 -

- 6 -

- 7 -

- 8 -

B·015

1. Mikey Burton / 2. André Beato / 3, 5. Hiekka Graphics / 4. Andrei D. Robu / 6. Dirty Little Secret / 7. The Original Champions of Design / 8. Rina Miele

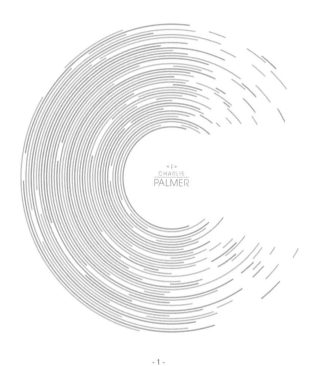

- 1 -

THE SYSTEM

- 2 -

The
Social
Learning
System

- 3 -

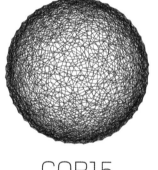

COP15
COPENHAGEN
UNITED NATIONS CLIMATE CHANGE CONFERENCE 2009

- 4 -

1. Mirko Ilic Corp. / 2. The KDU / 3. Manual / 4. NR2154

GRAPHIC ICON	GEOMETRY	ANIMATE	CIRCLE : DETAILED	POLYGON
LOGOTYPE	ABSTRACT	LIFESTYLE	QUADRILATERAL	
	EMBLEM	VEGETATION	TRIANGLE	

- 1 -

- 2 -

- 3 -

 FORMFIRE GLASSWORKS

 FORMFIRE GLASSWORKS

FORMFIRE GLASSWORKS

 FORMFIRE GLASSWORKS

 FORMFIRE GLASSWORKS

 FORMFIRE GLASSWORKS

- 4 -

B·017

1. Bless Ltd / 2. Ptarmak, Inc. / 3. Bo Lundberg, Jan Cafourek / 4. Corey Holms

- 1 -

- 2 -

- 3 -

- 4 -

- 5 -

- 6 -

- 7 -

- 8 -

- 9 -

1. Homework / 2. gardens&co. / 3. Joerg Merz / 4. Face. / 5. Cardon Webb / 6. Qube Studio / 7. Mucho / 8. Annika Kaltenthaler / 9. TOYKYO, Kaiser

FACTORY
HOTEL

- 1 -

MicroPlace

- 2 -

W●●●NDERLAND

- 3 -

AEOLAS
INTERNATIONAL

- 4 -

Fotografiska

- 5 -

ip connectz.

- 6 -

MΛIK

- 7 -

FORESTLAND
1967

- 8 -

ARKA
PHOTO

- 9 -

1. HelloMe™ / 2. Attik / 3. &Larry / 4. Alex Cornell / 5. BankerWessel / 6. TomTor Studio™ / 7. Mathias Ambus Studio / 8. Astronaut / 9. Olivier Courbet

GRAPHIC ICON	GEOMETRY	ANIMATE	CIRCLE : ABOVE THE NAME	POLYGON
LOGOTYPE	ABSTRACT	LIFESTYLE	QUADRILATERAL	
	EMBLEM	VEGETATION	TRIANGLE	

- 1 -

- 2 -

- 3 -

- 4 -

- 5 -

- 6 -

- 7 -

- 8 -

- 9 -

GRAPHIC ICON	GEOMETRY	ANIMATE	CIRCLE : ABOVE THE NAME	POLYGON
LOGOTYPE	ABSTRACT	LIFESTYLE	QUADRILATERAL	
	EMBLEM	VEGETATION	TRIANGLE	

- 1 -

- 2 -

- 3 -

- 4 -

- 5 -

- 6 -

- 7 -

- 8 -

- 9 -

B-021

- 1 -

- 2 -

- 3 -

- 4 -

- 5 -

- 6 -

- 7 -

- 8 -

1. DC / 2. Jolby / 3. Aloof Design / 4, 8. Eighth Day Design / 5. Tank Design / 6. 38one, LLC / 7. Purpose

GRAPHIC ICON	GEOMETRY	ANIMATE	CIRCLE : BY THE NAME	POLYGON
LOGOTYPE	ABSTRACT	LIFESTYLE	QUADRILATERAL	
	EMBLEM	VEGETATION	TRIANGLE	

- 1 -

- 2 -

- 3 -

- 4 -

- 5 -

- 6 -

- 7 -

- 8 -

B·023

- 1 -

- 2 -

B·024

1. Proud Creative / 2. Make®

- 1 -

- 2 -

- 3 -

- 4 -

- 5 -

- 6 -

- 7 -

- 8 -

1, 2. cypher13 / 3. StudioMakgill / 4. TomTor Studio™ / 5. Lucas Rampazzo / 6. James Davis / 7. Professor / 8. Peter Sunna

- 1 -

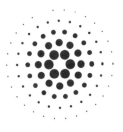

- 2 -

- 3 -

- 4 -

B·026

1. m Barcelona / 2. Giovanni Paletta "Krghettojuice" / 3. Studio Brave / 4. Dazld

Kulturhauptstadt Europas
RUHR.2010

- 1 -

- 2 -

- 3 -

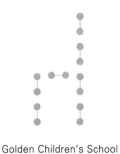

Golden Children's School

- 4 -

1. Fons Hickmann m23 / 2. BE COCO / 3. 38one, LLC / 4. Taste Inc.

GRAPHIC ICON	GEOMETRY	ANIMATE		CIRCLE : MONTAGE	POLYGON
LOGOTYPE	ABSTRACT	LIFESTYLE		QUADRILATERAL	
	EMBLEM	VEGETATION		TRIANGLE	

- 1 -

- 2 -

1. Craig & Karl / 2. Since 1416, graphic design & visual research

MASTERPEACE

MASTERPEACE

MASTERPEACE

MASTERPEACE

MASTERPEACE

MASTERPEACE

MASTERPEACE

- 1 -

- 2 -

- 3 -

- 4 -

- 5 -

- 6 -

- 7 -

- 8 -

- 9 -

1. Parent / 2. Mash Creative / 3. Studio Brave / 4. Made By Heath Killen / 5. Annika Kaltenthaler / 6. NNSS / 7. Chris Trivizas / 8. DixonBaxi / 9. Iconologic

- 1 -

- 2 -

- 3 -

- 4 -

- 5 -

- 6 -

- 7 -

- 8 -

- 9 -

B-031

1. Hiekka Graphics / 2. Mary-go-Round / 3. Eido Gat Graphic Design / 4. Office vs Office / 5. Daniel Portuga / 6. Megan Cummins / 7. NNSS /
8. TomTor Studio™ / 9. REX

- 1 -

- 2 -

- 3 -

- 4 -

- 5 -

- 6 -

- 7 -

- 8 -

1. H2 Design of Texas / 2. cypher13 / 3, 5, 7. Kern02 graphic design / 4. Dav Design/ed / 6. NunoMartins.com Design / 8. Paperjam Design Ltd.

המרכז לאורח חיים בריא

בריא אורח חיים במרכז

- 1 -

- 2 -

B·033

1. Michael Golan, Nadav Barkan / 2. Base Design Brussels

GRAPHIC ICON	GEOMETRY	ANIMATE	CIRCLE	POLYGON
LOGOTYPE	ABSTRACT	LIFESTYLE	QUADRILATERAL	
	EMBLEM	VEGETATION	TRIANGLE	

- 1 -

DESIGN4RENT

- 2 -

- 3 -

1. Form® / 2. Since 1416, graphic design & visual research / 3. Ariane Spanier Design

- 1 -

- 2 -

- 3 -

- 4 -

- 5 -

- 6 -

B•035

1. Áron Jancsó / 2. The Tenfold Collective / 3, 6. EMPK ATELIER / A / 4. QUSQUS / 5. Larimie Garcia

GRAPHIC ICON	GEOMETRY	ANIMATE	CIRCLE	POLYGON
LOGOTYPE	ABSTRACT	LIFESTYLE	QUADRILATERAL	
	EMBLEM	VEGETATION	TRIANGLE	

- 1 -

- 2 -

- 3 -

- 4 -

- 5 -

BLUE RUBICON

- 6 -

Faction North

- 7 -

RNAi

- 8 -

- 9 -

B·036

1. Face. / 2. Another Limited Rebellion / 3. JJAAKK / 4. Made Agency / 5. Stoëmp Studio / 6. R Design / 7. UNIT / 8. PMKFA / 9. Purpose

panaform™

- 1 -

WALKER

TRIBECA

- 2 -

- 3 -

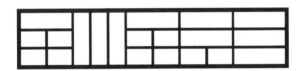

- 4 -

- 5 -

- 6 -

- 7 -

B·037

1, 3. TomTor Studio™ / 2. Oak / 4, 5. Vik LLC / 6, 7. Whitespace

GRAPHIC ICON	GEOMETRY	ANIMATE	CIRCLE	POLYGON
LOGOTYPE	ABSTRACT	LIFESTYLE	QUADRILATERAL	
	EMBLEM	VEGETATION	TRIANGLE	

- 1 -

- 2 -

- 3 -

- 4 -

- 5 -

- 6 -

- 7 -

1. Adam Morris / 2. Hazen Creative, Inc. / 3. Dazld / 4. Commando Group AS / 5. StudioKxx / 6. Mastronardi / Los Patos / 7. Faruk Akin

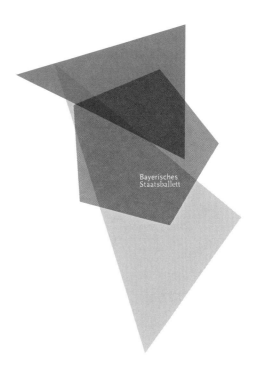

- 1 -

- 2 -

- 3 -

1. Fons Hickmann m23 / 2. Eido Gat Graphic Design / 3. Creuna

- 1 -

- 2 -

- 3 -

- 4 -

- 5 -

- 6 -

- 7 -

- 8 -

- 9 -

1, 2, 3. Bianca Wendt Ltd. / 4. StudioAnti™ / 5, 6. David Barath Design / 7, 8. Wink, Incorporated / 9. ICE CREAM FOR FREE™

- 1 -

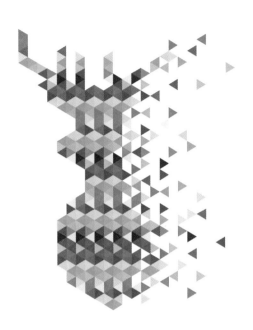

- 2 -

MINISTERSTWO
SPRAW
ZAGRANICZNYCH
WSPÓŁPRACA Z POLONIĄ

- 3 -

B·041

1. Nathan Brunstein / 2. Liam Randall / 3. Super Super

RECORDS

- 1 -

BLACK DIAMOND
STUDIO

- 3 -

L. M.
TILMAN & CO.
The Science of Value Creation℠

- 4 -

PENGRETA
TECHNOLOGY
INC.

- 5 -

OPTICAL ILLUSIONS

WORK & PLAY
EST. 2006

- 2 -

DESIGN
FOR
ENTERPRISES

- 6 -

1. Maxime Delporte / 2. Mark Brunswicker / 3. EMPK ATELIER / A / 4. Topos Graphics / 5. Alek Chmura / 6. Couple

- 1 -

- 2 -

- 3 -

- 4 -

- 5 -

1. Joerg Merz / 2. Frank Rocholl / 3. Mikey Burton / 4. Brighten The Corners / 5. ICG (Intereurope Communications Group)

GRAPHIC ICON	GEOMETRY	ANIMATE	COLOUR PRIMARIES	LINES & CURVES
LOGOTYPE	ABSTRACT	LIFESTYLE	PATTERN	
	EMBLEM	VEGETATION	SYMMETRY	

- 1 -

- 2 -

- 3 -

- 4 -

- 5 -

- 6 -

EDIFÍCIODOPARQUE

- 7 -

- 8 -

- 9 -

B-044

1, 2, 9. NNSS / 3. Vijf890 Ontwerpers / 4, 5. Guillaume Kashima / 6. JECT / 7. NunoMartins.com Design / 8. VONSUNG

B-045

- 1 -

- 2 -

- 3 -

- 4 -

- 5 -

B·046

1, 2. Duffy & Partners / 3. Claire Concept & Design / 4. Swivelhead Design Works, LLC / 5. Stylism

- 1 -

- 2 -

- 3 -

- 4 -

- 5 -

- 6 -

klickr

- 7 -

sonyworld

- 8 -

B•047

1. Since 1416, graphic design & visual research / 2. 38one, LLC / 3. Mastronardi / Los Patos / 4. TomTor Studio™ /
5. Graphic design studio by Yurko Gutsulyak / 6. Creuna / 7. Ontwerpstudio ttwwoo / 8. Frank Rocholl

baltic music

- 1 -

WAYPOINT

AT POULTON PLAIZ

- 2 -

POULTON
PLAIZ

HOLIDAY PARK

- 3 -

Sitges Vila de festivals

- 4 -

Eurobiotherm
BIOMASS ENERGY

- 5 -

ICON.

- 6 -

- 7 -

CONTEMPORARY ART MANCHESTER

- 8 -

Isvara
FOUNDATION

- 9 -

B·048

1. DADADA studio / 2, 3. ICG (Intereurope Communications Group) / 4. Marnich Associates / 5. Jaek el diablo / 6. Attik / 7. Lundgren+Lindqvist /
8. G-MAN / 9. Inksurge

- 1 -

- 2 -

- 3 -

- 4 -

- 5 -

- 6 -

- 7 -

- 8 -

- 9 -

B-049

TheColorRepublic

- 1 -

You Can Thrive!
FOUNDATION

*Rhythm*Thrive!

*Eco*Thrive!

- 2 -

B·050

1. Since 1416, graphic design & visual research / 2. Oak

- 1 -

- 2 -

B·051

1. NotJones Design / 2. Graphical House

DIGNITY

DIGNITY

DIGNITY

DIGNITY

DIGNITY

DIGNITY

DIGNITY

DIGNITY

DIGNITY

Barnbrook

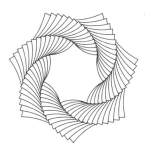

THE CHICAGO SPIRE

INSPIRED BY NATURE
IMAGINED BY CALATRAVA

- 1 -

BALTAYAN™

- 2 -

SILKEWEGGEN™

- 3 -

NALINDESIGN™

- 4 -

- 5 -

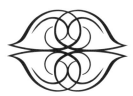

- 6 -

CHARTER CLUB®

- 7 -

B·053

- 1 -

- 2 -

- 3 -

- 4 -

- 5 -

- 6 -

- 7 -

- 8 -

- 9 -

1. ICG (Intereurope Communications Group) / 2. Mind Design / 3. Jeffrey Docherty, Kevin Wolahan / 4. Jee-eun Lee / 5. Jee-eun Lee, Yona Lee / 6. Attik /
7. Fontan 2 / 8. Draplin Design Co. / 9. DC

GRAPHIC ICON	GEOMETRY	ANIMATE	COLOUR PRIMARIES	LINES & CURVES
LOGOTYPE	**ABSTRACT**	LIFESTYLE	PATTERN	
	EMBLEM	VEGETATION	**SYMMETRY**	

- 1 -

- 2 -

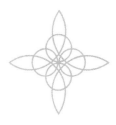

- 3 -

WITTLINGER HAHN STERN
RADIOLOGEN

- 4 -

Amsterdam

- 5 -

- 6 -

- 7 -

- 8 -

- 9 -

1. Parent / 2. Attik / 3. Foreign Policy Design Group / 4. Ippolito Fleitz Group GmbH / 5. Calango / 6. Whitespace / 7. The KDU / 8. Mirko Ilic Corp. /
9. NNSS

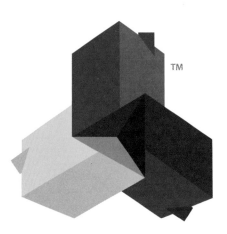

- 1 -

- 2 -

- 3 -

- 4 -

- 5 -

- 6 -

1. Richard Baird / 2. Studio MIKMIK / 3. Hazen Creative, Inc. / 4. Swivelhead Design Works, LLC / 5. Glitz Design / 6. ICG (Intereurope Communications Group)

GRAPHIC ICON	GEOMETRY	ANIMATE	COLOUR PRIMARIES	LINES & CURVES
LOGOTYPE	**ABSTRACT**	LIFESTYLE	PATTERN	
	EMBLEM	VEGETATION	**SYMMETRY**	

- 1 -

- 2 -

- 3 -

- 4 -

- 5 -

- 6 -

- 7 -

- 8 -

B-057

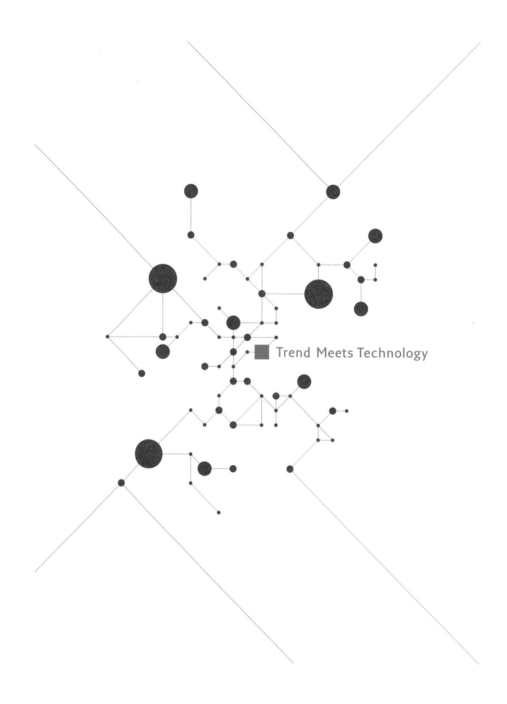

Trend Meets Technology

B·058

Shinnoske Design Inc.

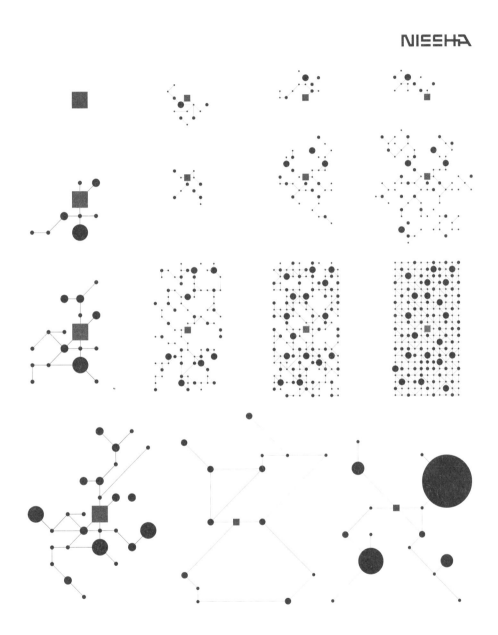

NIESHA

Shinnoske Design Inc.

DESIGN

- 1 -

MÜNCHNER
OPERNFESTSPIELE
2009

- 2 -

B·060

1. REX / 2. Fons Hickmann m23

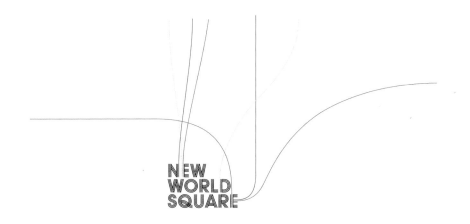

- 1 -

MORI ARTS CENTER

MORI ARTS CENTER

MORI ARTS CENTER

MORI ARTS CENTER

MORI ARTS CENTER

MORI ARTS CENTER

- 2 -

B·061

- 1 -

- 2 -

- 3 -

- 4 -

- 5 -

- 6 -

- 7 -

- 8 -

1. Ptarmak, Inc. / 2. ICG (Intereurope Communications Group) / 3. DC / 4. Foreign Policy Design Group / 5. The Tenfold Collective / 6. Hiekka Graphics /
7, 8. Iconologic

- 1 -

- 2 -

- 3 -

- 4 -

- 5 -

B·063

1. Jeffrey Docherty / 2. Decoylab Design Studio / 3. Electrofork / 4. The Creative Method / 5. Hiekka Graphics

- 1 -

- 2 -

- 3 -

- 4 -

- 5 -

- 6 -

1. Iconblast (Victor Ortiz G.) / 2. Urban Influence / 3, 4. Thunderdog Studios, Inc. / 5. Electrofork / 6. the Beautiful Design, Inc.

- 1 -

- 2 -

- 3 -

- 4 -

1. Sussner Design Company / 2. VONSUNG / 3. The Chase / 4. Glauco Diogenes Design Ltd

- 1 -

- 2 -

- 3 -

- 4 -

1. Face. / 2. Cardon Webb / 3, 4. Schwartz & Sons

- 1 -

- 2 -

- 3 -

- 4 -

- 5 -

B•067

B·068

- 1 -

- 2 -

- 3 -

- 4 -

- 5 -

- 6 -

- 7 -

- 8 -

- 9 -

B·069

- 1 -

- 2 -

- 3 -

- 4 -

- 5 -

- 6 -

- 7 -

- 8 -

- 9 -

1. TomTor Studio™ / 2, 6. the Beautiful Design, Inc. / 3. Jonathan Sandridge / 4. The Tenfold Collective / 5. NALINDESIGN / 7. Duffy & Partners /
8. Richard Stott / 9. Steven Bonner

- 1 -

- 2 -

- 3 -

- 4 -

- 5 -

- 6 -

- 7 -

- 8 -

- 9 -

1. Gavin Taylor / 2. the Beautiful Design, Inc. / 3. Draplin Design Co. / 4. Jonathan Sandridge / 5. Superatelier / 6. Proud Creative / 7. Ptarmak, Inc. /
8. Bless Ltd / 9. Royalefam Pte Ltd

- 1 -

- 2 -

- 3 -

- 4 -

- 5 -

- 6 -

- 7 -

B•072

- 1 -

- 2 -

ABSOLUTE BUILDERS

- 3 -

B•073

1, 2. forcefeed:swede / 3. the Beautiful Design, Inc.

- 1 -

- 2 -

- 3 -

- 4 -

- 5 -

- 6 -

SALINAS LASHERAS

NEO ARCHITECTURE

- 7 -

- 8 -

B·074

1. Rubber Design / 2. Marque Creative / 3, 5. H2 Design of Texas / 4. Daniel Portuga / 6. Przemek Ostaszewski / 7. Face. / 8. Mathias Martin

GRAPHIC ICON	GEOMETRY	ANIMATE	INSECTS	MAMMALS
LOGOTYPE	ABSTRACT	LIFESTYLE	FOWLS	HUMAN
	EMBLEM	VEGETATION	MARINE LIFE	

- 1 -

RX
SKIN CLINIC

- 2 -

- 3 -

B·075

1. Turnstyle / 2. Megan Cummins / 3. Stylo Design

euforia

- 1 -

EAGLECLEAN

- 2 -

GABRIELA ROMERO

CULINARY ADVISOR

- 3 -

- 4 -

absolut

- 5 -

ROYAL CHEAP$KATE

- 6 -

perch

- 7 -

BLUEBIRD

- 8 -

- 9 -

1. Commando Group AS / 2. The Partners / 3. Face. / 4. Make® / 5. Annika Kaltenthaler / 6. Ian Lynam Design / 7. Rubber Design / 8. Astronaut / 9. NNSS

- 1 -

bluebird C A F E

- 2 -

- 3 -

- 4 -

- 5 -

- 6 -

- 7 -

- 8 -

- 9 -

B·077

- 1 -

- 2 -

- 3 -

- 4 -

- 5 -

1. Mikey Burton / 2. Decoylab Design Studio / 3. One Trick Pony / 4. Graphical House / 5. Ian Lynam Design

- 1 -

- 2 -

- 3 -

- 4 -

- 5 -

- 6 -

- 7 -

- 8 -

- 9 -

B-079

GRAPHIC ICON	GEOMETRY	ANIMATE		INSECTS	MAMMALS
LOGOTYPE	ABSTRACT	LIFESTYLE		FOWLS	HUMAN
	EMBLEM	VEGETATION		MARINE LIFE	

- 1 -

- 2 -

- 3 -

- 4 -

- 5 -

- 6 -

- 7 -

- 8 -

B•080

1. A3 Design, LLC / 2. Truly Design / 3. Automatic Art and Design / 4. Ontwerpstudio ttwwoo / 5. Imagebox Productions, Inc. / 6. Nod Young /
7. Annika Kaltenthaler / 8. Studio Lin

- 1 -

- 2 -

- 3 -

- 4 -

- 5 -

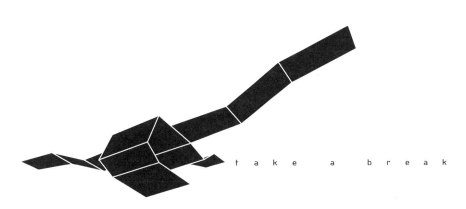

- 6 -

B-081

1. Super Super / 2. Studio Output / 3. Good Morning Design / 4. Nazario Graziano Studio / 5. H2 Design of Texas / 6. robotalex

- 1 -

- 2 -

- 3 -

- 4 -

FROG PRINCE

- 5 -

- 6 -

- 7 -

- 8 -

- 9 -

1. A3 Design, LLC / 2. Rubber Design / 3. DC / 4. Hazen Creative, Inc. / 5. Tamer Design & Direction / 6. Huschang Pourian / 7. TAKECARE /
8. TomTor Studio™ / 9. Alex Cornell

GRAPHIC ICON	GEOMETRY	ANIMATE	INSECTS	MAMMALS
LOGOTYPE	ABSTRACT	LIFESTYLE	FOWLS	HUMAN
	EMBLEM	VEGETATION	MARINE LIFE	

Odaku Sushi

- 1 -

- 2 -

vancouver
aquarium

- 3 -

FISH TRANSPORT

- 4 -

PATHOS

- 5 -

oceanus
RESEARCH GROUP

- 6 -

snail mail

- 7 -

<*))>{
CodeFish

- 8 -

B·083

- 1 -

- 2 -

- 3 -

- 4 -

- 5 -

- 6 -

1. Paperjam Design Ltd. / 2, 6. Sussner Design Company / 3. Imagebox Productions, Inc. / 4. FUN is OK / 5. Tomato Košir

- 1 -

- 2 -

- 3 -

- 4 -

- 5 -

- 6 -

- 7 -

- 8 -

- 9 -

B-085

1, 2. Draplin Design Co. / 3. Ian Lynam Design / 4. Daniel Flösser / 5. Studio Lin / 6. Made By Thomas / 7. Mikey Burton / 8, 9. Guillaume Kashima

- 1 -

- 2 -

- 3 -

- 4 -

- 5 -

- 6 -

- 7 -

- 8 -

- 9 -

1. Made By Heath Killen / 2. Marcus King / 3. biaugust CREATION OFFICE / 4. Lee Goater Design / 5. Ah&Oh Studio / 6. Iconologic / 7. Draplin Design Co. /
8. Manic Design / 9. TomTor Studio™

- 1 -

- 2 -

- 3 -

- 4 -

- 5 -

- 6 -

- 7 -

- 8 -

- 9 -

1. Proud Creative / 2. NNSS / 3. Office vs Office / 4. Via Grafik / 5. Gazelle Communication / 6. the Beautiful Design, Inc. / 7. TAKECARE / 8. Alex Cornell /
9. Mikael Fløysand, Julie Elise Hauge

TALL TALES
REAL FOOD

- 1 -

Aesmac.

- 2 -

komplet

- 3 -

A LIFELIKE ROBOT IMPOSTOR

- 4 -

FauxPink

- 5 -

- 6 -

REBELSOULRECORDS.

- 7 -

- 8 -

- 9 -

1. Duffy & Partners / 2. Face. / 3. Made Agency / 4. Studio On Fire / 5. Paul Tooth / 6. JJAAKK / 7. TomTor Studio™ / 8. Fons Hickmann m23 /
9. One Man's Studio

- 1 -

- 2 -

- 3 -

- 4 -

- 5 -

- 6 -

SONI
SOK Z noni TAHITI
946mL

- 7 -

- 8 -

- 9 -

1. Tim Boelaars / 2. Nod Young / 3. Sussner Design Company / 4. André Beato / 5. Hazen Creative, Inc. / 6. Bo Lundberg, Jan Cafourek / 7. Ah&Oh Studio /
8. Propel Group / 9. Herburg Weiland

- 1 -

- 2 -

- 3 -

- 4 -

- 5 -

- 6 -

- 7 -

- 8 -

- 9 -

1, 9. Wink, Incorporated / 2. Happy Lovers Town / 3. Needle Design & Illustration / 4. Bless Ltd / 5. Mikey Burton / 6. BERG / 7. Made By Thomas /
8. Antoine Corbineau

- 1 -

- 2 -

- 3 -

- 4 -

- 5 -

- 6 -

- 7 -

- 8 -

- 9 -

1. we are the future / 2. think simple act simple. / 3. Draplin Design Co. / 4. Kutchibok Limited / 5. Ivan Khmelevsky / 6. Bless Ltd / 7. Áron Jancsó /
8. Ontwerpstudio ttwwoo / 9. Swivelhead Design Works, LLC

- 1 -

- 2 -

- 3 -

B-093

1. Studio Volk™ / 2. Work By Stu / 3. Negro™

U.S. VIRGIN ISLANDS℠

st.CROIX   st.JOHN   st.THOMAS

st.JOHN℠
U.S. VIRGIN ISLANDS

st.THOMAS℠
U.S. VIRGIN ISLANDS

st.CROIX℠
U.S. VIRGIN ISLANDS

Iconologic

GRAPHIC ICON	GEOMETRY	ANIMATE	INSECTS	MAMMALS
LOGOTYPE	ABSTRACT	LIFESTYLE	FOWLS	HUMAN : FIGURE
	EMBLEM	VEGETATION	MARINE LIFE	

- 1 -

- 2 -

- 3 -

- 4 -

- 5 -

- 6 -

- 7 -

- 8 -

- 9 -

B·095

1. Jeffrey Docherty / 2. Rice 5 / 3. Justin Colt / 4. Mœ / 5. Frank Rocholl / 6. Mastronardi / Los Patos / 7. Iconologic /
8. Giovanni Paletta "Krghettojuice" / 9. Make®

- 1 -

- 2 -

- 3 -

- 4 -

1. Studio Fla / 2. PMKFA / 3. Vijf890 Ontwerpers / 4. Designbolaget

- 1 -

- 2 -

- 3 -

- 4 -

- 5 -

- 6 -

B-097

1. Faruk Akin / 2. Schwartz & Sons / 3. Cako Martin, Young & Rubicam Brazil / 4. The Original Champions of Design / 5. the Beautiful Design, Inc. / 6. NNSS

GRAPHIC ICON	GEOMETRY	ANIMATE	INSECTS	MAMMALS
LOGOTYPE	ABSTRACT	LIFESTYLE	FOWLS	HUMAN : FIGURE
	EMBLEM	VEGETATION	MARINE LIFE	

Savier Man ™

- 1 -

Savier Woman ™

- 2 -

- 3 -

- 4 -

B·098

1, 2. TomTor Studio™ / 3. Fons Hickmann m23 / 4. TOYKYO, Pointdextr

- 1 -

- 2 -

- 3 -

- 4 -

B·099

1. Lifter Baron / 2. Gee + Chung Design / 3. Needle Design & Illustration / 4. Jessica Keintz, Ross Bruggink

- 1 -

- 2 -

- 3 -

- 4 -

B·100

1. Happy Lovers Town / 2. Wink, Incorporated / 3. think simple act simple. / 4. DEMIAN CONRAD DESIGN

- 1 -

- 2 -

- 3 -

- 4 -

1. Codefrisko / 2. mousegraphics / 3. Unstru / 4. The Creative Method

- 1 -

- 2 -

- 3 -

- 4 -

- 5 -

1. Gianni Rossi Studio / 2. Made By Thomas / 3. Nod Young / 4. Studio Brito78 / 5. Gavin Taylor

B·103

biaugust

- 1 -

- 2 -

- 3 -

- 4 -

1. biaugust CREATION OFFICE / 2. Koshi Kawachi / 3. RADIO / 4. MessyMsxi

- 1 -

- 2 -

- 3 -

- 4 -

- 5 -

1. Ah&Oh Studio / 2, 4, 5. André Beato / 3. think simple act simple.

- 1 -

- 2 -

- 3 -

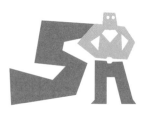

- 4 -

- 5 -

- 6 -

- 7 -

- 8 -

- 9 -

1. Julmeme / 2. DESIGN ARMY / 3. ReStart Associates / 4. Mikey Burton / 5. Ah&Oh Studio / 6. Alek Chmura / 7. Just Smile And Wave / 8. Method /
9. Guillaume Kashima

- 1 -

- 2 -

- 3 -

- 4 -

- 5 -

- 6 -

- 7 -

- 8 -

B·107

1. Ah&Oh Studio / 2. TOYKYO, Pointdextr / 3. André Beato / 4. Tamer Design & Direction / 5. Olli Hannonen / 6. cypher13 / 7. Negro™ / 8. Studio „The Form"

FLEUR

OGRA

KONKI

SAM

JET

GUS

PHILIPPE

DOYL+LOYD

- 1 -

- 2 -   - 3 -   - 4 -

- 5 -   - 6 -   - 7 -

1. JECT / 2. viction:workshop ltd. / 3, 4. Menta / 5. Lifter Baron / 6, 7. TOYKYO, Pointdextr

- 1 -

- 2 -

- 3 -

- 4 -

- 5 -

1, 2, 3. KLEE Concept & Creatie / 4. Design Ranch / 5. Tad Carpenter

AIC FOUNDATION

- 1 -

amarelo LINGERIE

- 2 -

LOVE YOUR BROWS™
THE BEAUTIFUL YOU

- 3 -

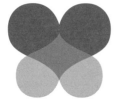

- 4 -

- 5 -

THE HEART
@MediaCityUK

- 6 -

- 7 -

- 8 -

- 9 -

1. Mirko Ilic Corp. / 2. Iconblast (Victor Ortiz G.) / 3, 6. Of Creative / 4. Hazen Creative, Inc. / 5. Toman Graphic Design / 7. Craig & Karl / 8. 38one, LLC /
9. FUN is OK

- 1 -

- 2 -

- 3 -

- 4 -

- 5 -

- 6 -

- 7 -

- 8 -

- 9 -

B·113

1. Studio Blanco / 2. DADADA studio / 3. HelloMe™ / 4. Fons Hickmann m23 / 5, 8. Lifter Baron / 6. Mike Abbink, Jordan Crane / 7. Dan Alexander & Co. / 9. ICE CREAM FOR FREE™

GRAPHIC ICON	GEOMETRY	ANIMATE	INSECTS	MAMMALS
LOGOTYPE	ABSTRACT	LIFESTYLE	FOWLS	HUMAN : HEART
	EMBLEM	VEGETATION	MARINE LIFE	

- 1 -

- 2 -

- 3 -

- 4 -

- 5 -

- 6 -

- 7 -

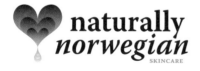

- 8 -

- 9 -

1. Stoëmp Studio / 2. Andrea Pippins / 3. ICG (Intereurope Communications Group) / 4. Chris Trivizas / 5. Janine Rewell / 6, 8. Claudia Graphic Design Studio /
7. DADADA studio / 9. Giovanni Paletta "Krghettojuice"

GRAPHIC ICON	GEOMETRY	ANIMATE	INSECTS	MAMMALS
LOGOTYPE	ABSTRACT	LIFESTYLE	FOWLS	HUMAN : EYE
	EMBLEM	VEGETATION	MARINE LIFE	

- 1 -

- 2 -

- 3 -

1. Iconblast (Victor Ortiz G.) / 2. Charlie Bouffart / 3. Tamer Design & Direction

- 1 -

- 2 -

- 3 -

- 4 -

- 5 -

- 6 -

- 7 -

- 8 -

1. Everything / 2, 3. Faruk Akin / 4. The Chase / 5. JECT, Mr Erik Tell / 6. Lifter Baron / 7. Dusan Jelesijevic / 8. Murillo Design, Inc.

- 1 -

- 2 -

- 3 -

1. Gianni Rossi Studio / 2. Murillo Design, Inc. / 3. Hazen Creative, Inc.

- 1 -

- 2 -

- 3 -

- 4 -

- 5 -

- 6 -

keito events

- 7 -

inno mind

- 8 -

1. R Design / 2. RDYA / 3. 38one, LLC / 4. GwlGraphisme / 5. Magpie Studio / 6. Form® / 7. Voice / 8. Hiekka Graphics

- 1 -

- 2 -

- 3 -

- 4 -

- 5 -

- 6 -

- 7 -

- 8 -

- 9 -

- 10 -

1. Zip Design Ltd. / 2. Glauco Diogenes Design Ltd / 3. cypher13 / 4. Give Up Art / 5. Mikey Burton / 6. Menta / 7. Studio „The Form" / 8. Benoit Lemoine / 9. FUN is OK / 10. ICG (Intereurope Communications Group)

- 1 -

- 2 -

- 3 -

- 4 -

- 5 -

- 6 -

- 7 -

- 8 -

- 9 -

1. Jaek el diablo / 2. Bruketa&Žinic OM / 3. Jessica Keintz / 4. Herburg Weiland / 5. Red Design Limited / 6. Magpie Studio / 7. Duffy & Partners /
8. The Tenfold Collective / 9. Subplot Design Inc.

GRAPHIC ICON	GEOMETRY	ANIMATE	INSECTS	MAMMALS
LOGOTYPE	ABSTRACT	LIFESTYLE	FOWLS	HUMAN : PALMS
	EMBLEM	VEGETATION	MARINE LIFE	

 TWO THOUSAND

 THREE THOUSAND

 FOUR THOUSAND

 FIVE THOUSAND

 SIX THOUSAND

- 1 -

UCDAVIS
FACILITIES
CARING FOR THE CAMPUS

UCDAVIS
OPERATIONS &
MAINTENANCE

UCDAVIS
ENVIRONMENTAL
HEALTH & SAFETY

UCDAVIS
ARCHITECTS &
ENGINEERS

UCDAVIS
FIRE
DEPARTMENT

UCDAVIS
INNOVATION &
QUALITY ASSURANCE

- 2 -

B·121

1. Craig & Karl / 2. Gee + Chung Design

- 1 -

- 2 -

- 3 -

- 4 -

- 5 -

1. Coba & Associates / 2. David R. Cornejo / 3. Studio Lin / 4. TomTor Studio™ / 5. Gavin Taylor

- 2 -

- 1 -

- 3 -

- 4 -

- 5 -

- 6 -

1. Proud Creative / 2. Tadas Karpavičius / 3. Bless Ltd / 4. The KDU / 5. Tim Boelaars / 6. Deuce Design

- 1 -

- 2 -

- 3 -

- 6 -

- 4 -

- 5 -

- 7 -

- 8 -

1. Studio MIKMIK / 2. Nod Young / 3. BY MASIF / 4. Turnstyle / 5. Gee + Chung Design / 6. BLOW / 7. Foreign Policy Design Group / 8. Whitespace

- 1 -

- 2 -

- 3 -

- 4 -

- 5 -

- 6 -

- 7 -

- 8 -

- 9 -

1. Celeste Prevost / 2, 6. inly products / 3. Oak / 4. Larimie Garcia / 5. Bless Ltd / 7. H2 Design of Texas / 8. the Beautiful Design, Inc. / 9. Joshua Wills

- 1 -

- 2 -

- 3 -

- 4 -

1. Iconologic / 2. We Are Ted / 3. Codefrisko / 4. Antoine Corbineau

- 1 -

- 2 -

- 3 -

- 4 -

- 5 -

- 6 -

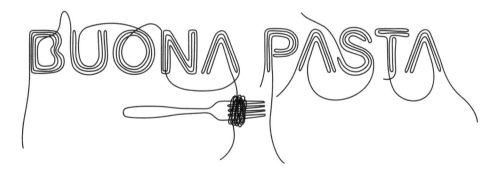

- 7 -

1. Automatic Art and Design / 2. Inksurge / 3. cypher13 / 4. the Beautiful Design, Inc. / 5. Salmon Design / 6. visualism | design & direction / 7. Losiento

- 1 -

- 2 -

- 3 -

- 4 -

- 5 -

- 6 -

- 7 -

- 8 -

- 9 -

1. Make® / 2. Studio Fla / 3. Chris Trivizas / 4. Tamer Design & Direction / 5. H2 Design of Texas / 6. Hazen Creative, Inc. / 7. Mastronardi / Los Patos /
8. Eytan Schiowitz Design / 9. DEMIAN CONRAD DESIGN

- 1 -

Mount **Pisgah**

- 2 -

- 3 -

- 4 -

- 5 -

- 6 -

STEM
AMBASSADORS
ILLUMINATING
FUTURES

- 7 -

1. Faruk Akin / 2. Dirty Little Secret / 3. Guillaume Kashima / 4. cypher13 / 5. Cardon Webb / 6. Negro™ / 7. Purpose

- 1 -

- 2 -

- 3 -

- 4 -

- 5 -

- 6 -

- 7 -

- 8 -

- 9 -

1. Nubby Twiglet / 2, 9. Magpie Studio / 3. José Antonio Contreras / 4. BE COCO / 5. Celeste Prevost / 6. Fontos Graphic Design Studio / 7. Jessica Keintz / 8. H2 Design of Texas

- 1 -

- 2 -

- 3 -

- 4 -

ST.2BOUTIQUES

- 5 -

- 6 -

- 7 -

- 8 -

1. Decoylab Design Studio / 2. Eytan Schiowitz Design / 3. Mikey Burton / 4. Samira Khoshnood / 5. Design Womb / Nicole LaFave / 6. Magpie Studio /
7. Electrofork / 8. Creasence

- 1 -

- 2 -

- 3 -

- 4 -

A Sound Fix

- 5 -

- 6 -

- 7 -

- 8 -

- 9 -

1. Graphic design studio by Yurko Gutsulyak / 2. Out of Order / 3. Chris Trivizas / 4. Murillo Design, Inc. / 5. Magpie Studio / 6. Studio Kluif /
7. Draplin Design Co. / 8. HelloMe™ / 9. Mastronardi / Los Patos

- 1 -

- 2 -

- 3 -

- 4 -

- 5 -

- 6 -

- 7 -

- 8 -

1. Needle Design & Illustration / 2. Out of Order / 3. Vijf890 Ontwerpers / 4. Magpie Studio / 5. Bruketa&Žinic OM / 6. André Beato / 7. Portas Design /
8. NNSS

- 1 -

- 2 -

- 3 -

- 4 -

- 5 -

- 6 -

- 7 -

- 8 -

- 9 -

1. Automatic Art and Design / 2. Wink, Incorporated / 3. Olivier Courbet / 4. Daniel Portuga / 5. Mikey Burton / 6. Josef Stapel / 7. WE RECOMMEND /
8. Mind Design / 9. Studio Brito78

- 1 -

- 2 -

- 3 -

- 4 -

- 5 -

- 6 -

- 7 -

- 8 -

- 9 -

B·135

1. Will Kinchin Graphic Design / 2. Nod Young / 3. Scandinavian Design Lab / 4. Murillo Design, Inc. / 5. Greg Christman / 6. Mikey Burton / 7. Studio Baer / 8. Melvin Galapon / 9. Purpose

- 1 -

- 2 -

- 3 -

- 4 -

- 5 -

- 6 -

- 7 -

1. Zip Design Ltd. / 2. G-MAN / 3. Chris Trivizas / 4. Plural / 5. Wink, Incorporated / 6. Automatic Art and Design / 7. Happy Lovers Town

CHÂTEAU DE BÉHOUST

- 1 -

West Penn Energy Solutions

- 2 -

- 3 -

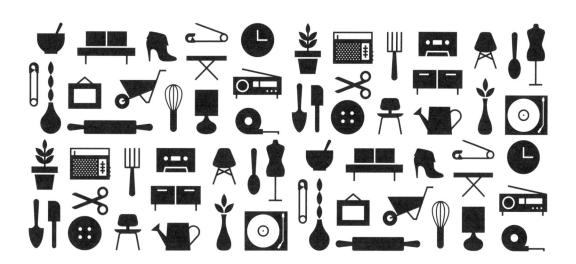

- 4 -

B•137

1. Benjamin Brard / 2. Imagebox Productions, Inc. / 3. Claudia Graphic Design Studio / 4. Celeste Prevost

- 1 -

- 2 -

- 3 -

- 4 -

- 5 -

- 6 -

1. The Tenfold Collective / 2. Schwartz & Sons / 3. Imagebox Productions, Inc. / 4. Lizette Gecel / 5, 6. Draplin Design Co.

- 1 -

- 2 -

- 3 -

- 4 -

- 5 -

- 6 -

- 7 -

- 8 -

- 9 -

1. BY MASIF / 2. Zion Graphics / 3. Studio Kluif / 4, 5. A3 Design, LLC / 6. Draplin Design Co. / 7, 9. Soulseven / 8. The Official Manufacturing Company

- 1 -

- 2 -

- 3 -

- 4 -

THINK LONDON

- 5 -

1. Urban Influence / 2. Chris Trivizas / 3, 4. Face. / 5. johnson banks

- 1 -

LINDEN HILLS
CO-OP
GROCERY & DELI

- 2 -

SQUARE MARKET

- 3 -

- 4 -

RAIL
HERITAGE
CENTRE
GO LOCO FOR A DAY

- 5 -

- 6 -

BENJAMIN BIXBY

- 7 -

Space Shuttle
1981 2010

- 8 -

FUEL
comics

- 9 -

1. Bruketa&Žinic OM / 2. Sussner Design Company / 3, 7. Iconologic / 4. Iconblast (Victor Ortiz G.) / 5. The Creative Method / 6. Ekaluck Peanpanawate / 8. Draplin Design Co. / 9. Alek Chmura

AMERICA'S
NATURAL GAS
ALLIANCE

- 1 -

BLING

- 2 -

ADISTA

- 3 -

- 4 -

- 5 -

- 6 -

- 7 -

- 8 -

- 9 -

1. Iconologic / 2, 3. Bruketa&Žinic OM / 4. Annika Kaltenthaler / 5. Whitespace / 6. Kanella / 7. Teldesign / 8. Louise Fili Ltd. / 9. Glauco Diogenes Design Ltd

DREAM
center

- 1 -

QUIMICALIS

- 2 -

Beachdown
Festival

- 3 -

VILLAGE RIDGE

BOUTIQUE HOTEL

★ ★ ★ ★

- 4 -

NO
HYPE
FOR
ME

- 5 -

- 6 -

Skiv
TRIO.

- 7 -

BULDO

- 8 -

CLUSTERPHONIC

- 9 -

B·143

- 1 -

- 2 -

- 3 -

- 4 -

- 5 -

- 6 -

1. Herburg Weiland / 2. TomTor Studio™ / 3. Art of Faya / 4. Mikael Fløysand, Anja Søvik, Argjend Nicki, Dennis Magnus-Andresen / 5. Oak / 6. Jaek el diablo

NORTH RIDGE
FILMS

- 1 -

DANTE LAYTON

- 2 -

- 3 -

spice mountain

- 4 -

- 5 -

B·145

1. Stylo Design / 2. Imagebox Productions, Inc. / 3. the Beautiful Design, Inc. / 4. Made by Thomas / 5. Draplin Design Co.

- 1 -

- 2 -

- 3 -

- 4 -

- 5 -

- 6 -

- 7 -

- 8 -

- 9 -

1. Dav Design/ed / 2. The Chase / 3. FUN is OK / 4. Celeste Prevost / 5, 6. This is Pacifica™ / 7. Electrofork / 8, 9. Olivier Courbet

GRAPHIC ICON	GEOMETRY	ANIMATE	FOLIAGE	WOOD
LOGOTYPE	ABSTRACT	LIFESTYLE	FRUITS	SILHOUETTE
	EMBLEM	VEGETATION	SCENERY	

- 1 -

- 2 -

- 3 -

- 4 -

- 5 -

- 6 -

- 7 -

- 8 -

- 9 -

B·147

1. Daniel Portuga / 2. BY MASIF / 3. Lizette Gecel / 4, 5. Bruketa&Žinic OM / 6. Made Agency / 7. Adam Morris / 8. Patricio Brito aka dznpuro* /
9. Joshua Wills

- 1 -

- 2 -

- 3 -

- 4 -

- 5 -

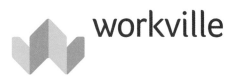

- 6 -

- 7 -

- 8 -

1. Stoëmp Studio / 2. Whitespace / 3. Nod Young / 4. Studio Ink / 5. Nazario Graziano Studio / 6. Creasence / 7. Jaek el diablo / 8. B&B studio

- 1 -

- 2 -

- 3 -

- 4 -

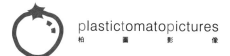

- 5 -

- 6 -

- 7 -

- 8 -

1. G-MAN / 2. Iconologic / 3. Whitespace / 4. Archerfish Studio Inc. / 5. robotalex / 6. Julmeme / 7. Larimie Garcia / 8. Mr. Tom Design

- 1 -

CONCEPTS

- 2 -

- 3 -

1. R Design / 2. KLEE Concept & Creatie / 3. Happy Lovers Town

GRAPHIC ICON	GEOMETRY	ANIMATE		FOLIAGE	WOOD
LOGOTYPE	ABSTRACT	LIFESTYLE		FRUITS	SILHOUETTE
	EMBLEM	VEGETATION		SCENERY	

- 1 -

- 2 -

1. Rubber Design / 2. Turnstyle

GRAPHIC ICON	GEOMETRY	ANIMATE	FOLIAGE	WOOD
LOGOTYPE	ABSTRACT	LIFESTYLE	FRUITS	SILHOUETTE
	EMBLEM	VEGETATION	SCENERY	

- 1 -

- 2 -

B·152

1. Mastronardi / Los Patos / 2. Studio Brave

ZAGRODA

- 1 -

- 2 -

- 3 -

1. Monika Ostaszewska-Olszewska, Przemek Ostaszewski / 2. Wink, Incorporated / 3. Lee Goater Design, Robert Cooper, Lowd&Klea

- 1 -

- 2 -

B·154

1. Rubber Design / 2. Whitespace

- 1 -

- 2 -

- 3 -

- 4 -

- 5 -

- 6 -

- 7 -

- 8 -

- 9 -

1. Decoylab Design Studio / 2. Dan Alexander & Co. / 3. Electrofork / 4. Portas Design / 5. Celeste Prevost / 6. H2 Design of Texas / 7. Studio Brito78 /
8. Studio MIKMIK / 9. Dusan Jelesijevic

- 1 -

The LEAVES COLLECTION
by Wissotzky

- 2 -

- 3 -

1. Ah&Oh Studio / 2. Dan Alexander & Co. / 3. Wink, Incorporated

- 1 -

- 2 -

- 3 -

- 4 -

- 5 -

- 6 -

- 7 -

- 8 -

- 9 -

1. Red Creative / 2. inly products / 3. Iconologic / 4. Bruketa&Žinic OM / 5. Kipi Ka Popo / 6. Portas Design / 7. Grzegorz Sołowiński /
8. Jonathan Gregory / 9. Asylum

- 1 -

WUNSCHBAUM

- 2 -

- 3 -

KAFFEEWEIZEN™

- 4 -

1, 4. NALINDESIGN / 2. Josef Stapel / 3. FUN is OK

- 1 -

- 2 -

- 3 -

- 4 -

- 5 -

- 6 -

- 7 -

- 8 -

MAS de la BASSEROLA

- 9 -

1. BrfDsgn / 2, 3. Huschang Pourian / 4, 5, 6. TomTor Studio™ / 7. Magpie Studio / 8. R Design / 9. espluga+associates

GRAPHIC ICON	INITIAL	STRUCTURAL	1 ALPHABET	4 ALPHABETS / CUBIC
LOGOTYPE	TYPE-ORIENTED	CHINESE CHARACTER	2 ALPHABETS	ABOVE THE NAME
	MASSIVE	ILLUSTRATIVE	3 ALPHABETS	BY THE NAME

- 1 -

- 2 -

- 3 -

- 4 -

- 5 -

- 6 -

- 7 -

- 8 -

- 9 -

1. Mucho / 2. Steven Bonner / 3. Jan Olof Nygren / 4. Bo Lundberg / 5. André Beato / 6. Alek Chmura / 7. Everything / 8. Annika Kaltenthaler / 9. Rudd Studio

- 1 -

- 2 -

- 3 -

- 4 -

- 5 -

- 6 -

- 7 -

- 8 -

- 9 -

B·161

1. Astronaut / 2. Studio Paradise / 3. Alex Perryman / 4. Coast Design / 5. Mash Creative / 6. Joerg Merz / 7. Dimo Trifonov / 8. Graphical House / 9. Chris Henley

- 1 -

- 2 -

- 3 -

- 4 -

- 5 -

- 6 -

- 7 -

- 8 -

- 9 -

1. Mash Creative / 2. Herburg Weiland / 3. DEMIAN CONRAD DESIGN / 4. Losiento / 5. Deuce Design / 6, 9. José Design&zo / 7. A Graphic Practice / 8. Everything

GRAPHIC ICON	**INITIAL**	STRUCTURAL	1 ALPHABET	4 ALPHABETS/CUBIC
LOGOTYPE	TYPE-ORIENTED	CHINESE CHARACTER	**2 ALPHABETS**	ABOVE THE NAME
	MASSIVE	ILLUSTRATIVE	3 ALPHABETS	BY THE NAME

- 1 -

- 2 -

- 3 -

- 4 -

- 5 -

- 6 -

- 7 -

- 8 -

- 9 -

B·163

1. Studio „The Form" / 2. Face. / 3. mousegraphics / 4. Paul Tooth / 5. Soulseven, FAME / 6. Wayne Tang / 7. Stylism, AGH & Friends /
8. Brigada Creativa / 9. Salmon Design

- 1 -

- 2 -

- 3 -

- 4 -

- 5 -

- 6 -

- 7 -

- 8 -

- 9 -

B·164

1, 3. Negro™ / 2. Mucho / 4. Mirko Ilic Corp. / 5. Ontwerphaven / 6. THERE / 7. Graphical House / 8. One Man's Studio / 9. NNSS

- 1 -

- 2 -

- 3 -

- 4 -

- 5 -

- 6 -

- 7 -

- 8 -

- 9 -

1. Studio Volk™ / 2. Coast Design / 3. One Man's Studio / 4. Richard Baird, Lockwood Publishing / 5. Method / 6. Ian Lynam Design / 7. Proud Creative /
8. Art of Faya / 9. Qube Konstrukt

- 1 -

- 2 -

- 3 -

- 4 -

- 5 -

1. Hiekka Graphics / 2. Fabio Ongarato Design / 3. Made By Heath Killen / 4. Kutchibok Limited / 5. Graphical House

GRAPHIC ICON	INITIALS	STRUCTURAL	1 ALPHABET	4 ALPHABETS/CUBIC
LOGOTYPE	TYPE-ORIENTED	CHINESE CHARACTER	2 ALPHABETS	ABOVE THE NAME
	MASSIVE	ILLUSTRATIVE	3 ALPHABETS	BY THE NAME

- 1 -

- 2 -

- 3 -

- 4 -

- 5 -

- 6 -

- 7 -

- 8 -

- 9 -

B·167

1. BLOW / 2. Hiekka Graphics / 3. biaugust CREATION OFFICE / 4. Hazen Creative, Inc. / 5. 3group / 6. NNSS / 7. Tomato Košir / 8. Letterbox /
9. Eighth Day Design

GRAPHIC ICON	INITIAL	STRUCTURAL	1 ALPHABET	4 ALPHABETS/CUBIC
LOGOTYPE	TYPE-ORIENTED	CHINESE CHARACTER	2 ALPHABETS	**ABOVE THE NAME**
	MASSIVE	ILLUSTRATIVE	3 ALPHABETS	BY THE NAME

STUDIO/CREATIVO

- 1 -

VYACHESLAV
KIRILENKO

- 2 -

publishus

- 3 -

MUMFORDS LAWYERS

- 4 -

ARTISANALE
ATELIER

- 5 -

LOLA LONDON
PHOTOGRAPHY

- 6 -

Andreas Caminada

- 7 -

WIVENHOE

- 8 -

XELIO
print house

- 9 -

B·168

---

1. Nazario Graziano Studio / 2. Astronaut / 3. Dazld / 4. THERE / 5. QUSQUS / 6. Nubby Twiglet / 7. Remo Caminada, Michael Häne / 8. Paul Tooth / 9. Alek Chmura

- 1 -

- 2 -

- 3 -

- 4 -

- 5 -

- 6 -

- 7 -

- 8 -

B·169

1. Nod Young / 2. Remo Caminada, Michael Häne / 3. 38one, LLC / 4. Fontos Graphic Design Studio / 5. Hyperlocaldesign / 6. THERE /
7. Nazario Graziano Studio / 8. Astronaut

**AUTHENTIC
DESIGN ALLIANCE**
Supporting
Original Design

- 1 -

- 2 -

- 3 -

- 4 -

- 5 -

- 6 -

- 7 -

- 8 -

1. THERE / 2. Office vs Office / 3, 4. Tank Design / 5. Manual / 6. Alek Chmura / 7. David Barath Design / 8. Astronaut

- 1 -

- 2 -

- 3 -

- 4 -

- 5 -

- 6 -

- 7 -

- 8 -

B·171

1, 4, 7. Astronaut / 2. Peter Sunna / 3. THERE / 5. Qube Konstrukt / 6. gardens&co. / 8. StudioMakgill

- 1 -

- 2 -

- 3 -

- 4 -

- 5 -

- 6 -

- 7 -

B·172

1. Peter Sunna / 2. Stylism / 3, 5. Negro™ / 4. Astronaut / 6. Barbara Muriungi / 7. Grzegorz Sołowiński

ikonik™

- 1 -

nieformalnıe
Club & Lounge

- 2 -

nieformalnie
Club & Lounge

- 3 -

Fotografia

- 4 -

great.

- 5 -

vintage

- 6 -

luckipocki

- 7 -

walesɘ|ɐw

- 8 -

1. REX / 2, 3. Grzegorz Sołowiński / 4. Mads Burcharth / 5. Homework / 6. Astronaut / 7. BLOW / 8. Aloof Design

roppongi hills

roppongi hills

roppongi hills

roppongi hills

roppongi hills

roppongi hills

Barnbrook

base//estētica

- 1 -

grafika˙druk®

- 2 -

stillness silence

- 3 -

Mike&Maaike

- 4 -

Dafi/Academy

- 5 -

1. espluga+associates / 2. Alek Chmura / 3. NSSGRAPHICA / 4. Manual / 5. Homework

- 1 -

Édition 08

- 2 -

SPADA

- 3 -

- 4 -

PARLOR

- 5 -

- 6 -

BALANCE

- 7 -

1. Studio Output / 2. Akatre / 3. Studio Blanco / 4. Eighth Day Design / 5. RoAndCo Studio / 6. cypher13 / 7. Ryan Crouchman

Stockholm Oakland Design Group

- 1 -

AMSTERDAM

- 2 -

HALF FÚLL

- 3 -

VAAKA

PARTNERS

- 4 -

- 5 -

FES TLIP

FESTIVAL DE TEATRO DA LÍNGUA PORTUGUESA

- 6 -

- 7 -

research | planning | direction

- 8 -

1. Bo Lundberg / 2. José Design&zo / 3. StudioMakgill / 4. Hiekka Graphics / 5. Super Super / 6. Portas Design / 7. cypher13 / 8. Made Agency

FUTUREPLACE

- 1 -

OUTCAST™

- 2 -

DESIGNER COLLECTIVE

- 3 -

NARBRU

- 4 -

- 5 -

- 6 -

REPUBLIQUE

- 7 -

1. Marque Creative / 2. Vik LLC / 3. Stoëmp Studio / 4. Alexis Taleb / 5. Super Super / 6. Ian Lynam Design / 7. Scandinavian Design Lab

DUOHTA VUOHTA®

- 1 -

SOCIALTRADERS

- 2 -

TİMO.WEİLAND

- 3 -

C/O

THE MAIDSTONE

- 4 -

●.I.L. PRODUCTION™

Organized Interlink Production

- 5 -

B·179

1. Hiekka Graphics / 2. Fabio Ongarato Design / 3. RoAndCo Studio / 4. Letters & Numbers / 5. NSSGRAPHICA

- 1 -

- 2 -

- 3 -

- 4 -

- 5 -

- 6 -

- 7 -

- 8 -

1. Nôde Design / 2. Ben Cridland / 3. HelloMe™ / 4. Negro™ / 5. Steven Bonner / 6. Áron Jancsó / 7. B&W Studio / 8. viction:workshop ltd.

PAVE MENT GORI LLAZ

- 1 -

ORIGINAL®
KOLLECTIVE

- 2 -

maximall gallery

- 3 -

Swerdlow
Interiors.

- 4 -

MAJE. EN SCENE

- 5 -

ADF ARCHITECTS

- 6 -

primero primera

- 7 -

AIRBORNE ADVERTISING

- 8 -

1. George Strouzas / 2. André Beato / 3. Grzegorz Sołowiński / 4. Creative Spark / 5. Sara Haraigue / 6. Graphical House / 7. Mucho / 8. Nicknack

MARK ROPER
PHOTOGRAPHY

- 1 -

KOBUCHIZAWA
ART VILLAGE

- 2 -

annie
greenabelle

- 3 -

PHELPSANIMALS
PHELPSANIMALS

- 4 -

COPENHAGEN®
FASHIONWEEK

- 5 -

1. Salmon Design / 2. Hinterland, LLC / 3. Studio Output / 4. Charlie Hocking / 5. Homework

- 1 -

- 2 -

- 3 -

West
Webbe
+Accountancy

- 4 -

Ctrl+C

- 5 -

Kinsley
+Associates

- 6 -

CAFE+®
SPACE
BEYOND

- 7 -

Lundgren+Lindqvist™

- 8 -

1. Àxel Durana / 2. REX / 3. DC / 4. Hello Milo / 5. Studio Blanco / 6. 38one, LLC / 7. LOWORKS / 8. Lundgren+Lindqvist

- 1 -

NOOKA®

- 2 -

platform__

- 3 -

workspace³

- 4 -

m_lab

- 5 -

KONEKT

- 6 -

[EXPOSURƎ]

- 7 -

1. Mary-go-Round / 2. Nooka Inc. / 3. Homework / 4. Hiekka Graphics / 5. espluga+associates / 6. Alex Perryman / 7. de.MO design

Grip:

- 1 -

onebar™

- 2 -

:DIDOGO

- 3 -

MOLOKO

- 4 -

:Pelis chulas

- 5 -

- 6 -

ƎƐ:0I:SƐ!
PLATTFORM

- 7 -

- 8 -

1. Heydays / 2. Rubber Design / 3. Creasence / 4, 6. Grzegorz Sołowiński / 5. m Barcelona / 7. phospho / 8. Base Design New York

Mary Anne Hobbs

- 1 -

body boutique

- 2 -

- 3 -

- 4 -

Olyinka

- 5 -

SAUVAGE

UNTITLED

- 6 -

1, 3. Studio Output / 2. Zip Design Ltd. / 4. Fontan 2 / 5. Alex Perryman / 6. Richard Robinson

GRAPHIC ICON	INITIALS	STRUCTURAL		IN A ROW	LINE
LOGOTYPE	**TYPE-ORIENTED**	CHINESE CHARACTER		**MIXED : GRAPHICS**	CALLIGRAPHY
	MASSIVE	ILLUSTRATIVE		PALETTE	LETTERING

- 1 -

- 2 -

- 3 -

- 4 -

- 5 -

GREEN WOLF

- 6 -

- 7 -

1. Paul Tooth / 2. Mucho / 3. The Consult / 4, 7. Alex Chavot / 5. Iconblast (Victor Ortiz G.) / 6. Zip Design Ltd.

- 1 -

- 2 -

- 3 -

- 4 -

- 5 -

1, 5. Negro™ / 2, 3, 4. Studio Fla

- 1 -

- 2 -

- 3 -

- 4 -

- 5 -

- 6 -

- 7 -

- 8 -

- 9 -

B·189

1. Áron Jancsó / 2. Give Up Art / 3. Parent / 4. Studio Brave / 5. Adam Morris / 6. Neubau. / 7. DC / 8. Glitz design / 9. NNSS

FredericiaC

- 1 -

- 2 -

- 3 -

- 4 -

- 5 -

1. Make® / 2. FUN is OK / 3. NNSS / 4. Creative Spark / 5. Give Up Art, Adam Morten

GRAPHIC ICON	INITIALS	STRUCTURAL		IN A ROW	LINE
LOGOTYPE	**TYPE-ORIENTED**	CHINESE CHARACTER		MIXED	CALLIGRAPHY
	MASSIVE	ILLUSTRATIVE		**PALETTE : GRADATION**	LETTERING

- 1 -

- 2 -

- 3 -

- 4 -

- 5 -

- 6 -

- 7 -

- 8 -

B·191

1. Dolly Rogers / 2. Gazelle Communication / 3. Maldesign / 4. We love moules frites / 5. Nazario Graziano Studio / 6. The Creative Method /
7. Glitz design / 8. Frank Rocholl

GRAPHIC ICON	INITIALS	STRUCTURAL		IN A ROW	LINE
LOGOTYPE	TYPE-ORIENTED	CHINESE CHARACTER		MIXED	CALLIGRAPHY
	MASSIVE	ILLUSTRATIVE		PALETTE : OVERPRINT	LETTERING

- 1 -

- 2 -

- 3 -

- 4 -

1. Áron Jancsó / 2. Nicknack / 3. Glasfurd & Walker Design / 4. Forest

GRAPHIC ICON	INITIALS	STRUCTURAL
LOGOTYPE	**TYPE-ORIENTED**	CHINESE CHARACTER
	MASSIVE	ILLUSTRATIVE

IN A ROW	LINE
MIXED	CALLIGRAPHY
PALETTE : OVERPRINT	LETTERING

- 1 -

- 2 -

- 3 -

- 4 -

- 5 -

- 6 -

- 7 -

alitalia

- 8 -

1. Foreign Policy Design Group / 2. COLMO / 3. Studio Laucke / 4. Stylism / 5. Hafez Janssens Design / 6. A3 Design, LLC / 7. The KDU / 8. Wayne Tang

CITY OF MELBOURNE

CITY OF MELBOURNE

CITY OF MELBOURNE

CITY OF MELBOURNE

CITY OF MELBOURNE

CITY OF MELBOURNE

CITY OF MELBOURNE

CITY OF MELBOURNE

CITY OF MELBOURNE

CITY OF MELBOURNE

CITY OF MELBOURNE

CITY OF MELBOURNE

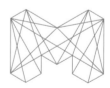

CITY OF MELBOURNE

Landor Associates Sydney

GRAPHIC ICON	INITIALS	STRUCTURAL		IN A ROW	LINE
LOGOTYPE	**TYPE-ORIENTED**	CHINESE CHARACTER		MIXED	CALLIGRAPHY
	MASSIVE	ILLUSTRATIVE		**PALETTE : VIBRANT**	LETTERING

- 1 -

- 2 -

- 3 -

- 4 -

- 5 -

1, 2, 3. Playful / 4, 5. Giedre Domzaite

- 1 -

- 2 -

- 3 -

- 4 -

- 5 -

- 6 -

1, 2. TOYKYO, Pointdextr / 3, 4, 5, 6. Fontan 2

GRAPHIC ICON	INITIALS	STRUCTURAL		IN A ROW	LINE
LOGOTYPE	**TYPE-ORIENTED**	CHINESE CHARACTER		MIXED	CALLIGRAPHY
MASSIVE		ILLUSTRATIVE		**PALETTE : VIBRANT**	LETTERING

- 1 -

thesoulproject.com

- 2 -

- 3 -

- 4 -

- 5 -

1. Nod Young / 2. Grzegorz Sołowiński / 3. Toman Graphic Design / 4. Studio Lin / 5. Wishart Design

- 1 -

- 2 -

1. Edhv / 2. Shinnoske Design Inc.

GRAPHIC ICON	INITIALS	STRUCTURAL		IN A ROW	LINE
LOGOTYPE	**TYPE-ORIENTED**	CHINESE CHARACTER		MIXED	CALLIGRAPHY
MASSIVE		ILLUSTRATIVE		**PALETTE : VIBRANT**	LETTERING

- 1 -

- 2 -

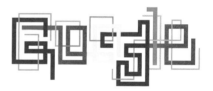

- 3 -

- 4 -

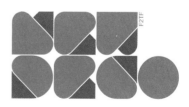

- 5 -

1, 2, 3. MWM Graphics / 4. ALVA® / 5. Fontan 2

- 1 -

KALEIDOSCOPE

- 2 -

- 3 -

1. David Barath Design / 2. Monika Ostaszewska / 3. Forest

GRAPHIC ICON	INITIALS	STRUCTURAL		IN A ROW	LINE
LOGOTYPE	**TYPE-ORIENTED**	CHINESE CHARACTER		MIXED	CALLIGRAPHY
MASSIVE		ILLUSTRATIVE		**PALETTE : VIBRANT**	LETTERING

Próximo Futuro / NexT Future

- 1 -

- 2 -

- 3 -

- 4 -

- 5 -

1, 2. ALVA® / 3. Mastronardi / Los Patos / 4. Dimo Trifonov / 5. Nod Young

- 1 -

- 2 -

- 3 -

- 4 -

1. Homework / 2. Nubby Twiglet / 3. Zip Design Ltd. / 4. EMPK ATELIER / A

- 1 -

- 2 -

- 3 -

- 4 -

B·203

1, 3. EMPK ATELIER / A / 2. Studio Fla / 4. Ontwerphaven

- 1 -

THE SATURDAYS

- 2 -

- 3 -

TiVo HD

- 4 -

ROUND

- 5 -

MIOVA

- 6 -

AVATAR

- 7 -

PAVEMENT

- 8 -

B-204

1. Moltefacce srl / 2. Zip Design Ltd. / 3. Ian Lynam Design / 4. Hafez Janssens Design / 5. Mads Burcharth / 6. Grzegorz Sołowiński /
7. Iconblast (Victor Ortiz G.) / 8. Made By Heath Killen

- 1 -

- 2 -

- 3 -

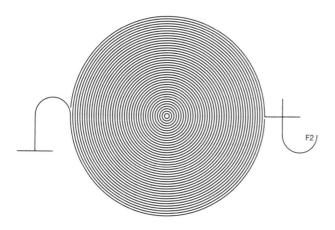

- 4 -

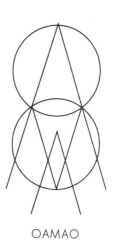

OAMAO

- 5 -

1. Áron Jancsó / 2, 4. Fontan 2 / 3. Mark Brunswicker / 5. HelloMe™

THE LOLLIPOP SHOPPE

- 1 -

connoisseur

- 2 -

Onpedder

- 3 -

Mölndals Cykelklubb

- 4 -

MOTHERNISM™

- 5 -

atomic attack

- 6 -

1. StudioMakgill / 2. viction:workshop ltd. / 3. Fabio Ongarato Design / 4. Jan Olof Nygren / 5. Studio Volk™ / 6. Atomic Attack

- 1 -

- 2 -

CROWN METROPOL

- 3 -

fluture

- 4 -

SEULGI LEE

- 5 -

DANCE CREW

- 6 -

L'ABATTOIR

- 7 -

1. Calango / 2. Oak / 3. Fabio Ongarato Design / 4. Lucas Rampazzo / 5. Akatre / 6. My Friend Pike / 7. Glasfurd & Walker Design

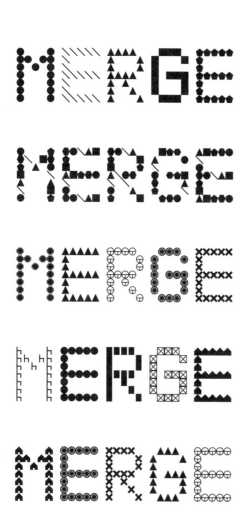

- 1 -

Nineteen Eighty Four

- 2 -

Nineteen Seventy Two

- 3 -

LOJA   SHOP

- 4 -

1. Studio Lin / 2, 3. Simon C Page / 4. This is Pacifica™

- 1 -

- 2 -

- 3 -

- 4 -

- 5 -

- 6 -

1, 5. Fontan 2 / 2. Calango / 3. G-MAN / 4. Negro™ / 6. The KDU

SATURDAY
STUDIO.

- 1 -

CHARLIE
HOCKING

- 2 -

KERN02
GRAFISCH
ONTWERP

- 3 -

  DUTCH INNOVATION CENTRE
FOR ELECTRIC ROAD TRANSPORT

- 4 -

1. Paul Tooth / 2. Charlie Hocking / 3. Kern02 graphic design / 4. DC

- 1 -

- 2 -

- 3 -

- 4 -

- 5 -

- 6 -

- 7 -

- 8 -

B·211

1. Frank Rocholl / 2. Moltefacce srl / 3. Face. / 4, 6, 8. Paul Tooth / 5. mousegraphics / 7. Grzegorz Sołowiński

- 1 -

- 2 -

- 3 -

1. NNSS / 2. NALINDESIGN / 3. forcefeed:swede

André Beato

- 1 -

- 2 -

- 3 -

- 4 -

- 5 -

1. The Creative Method / 2. Marnich Associates / 3. Face. / 4. visualism | design & direction / 5. Dirty Little Secret

ah&oh

- 1 -

t.schindler

- 2 -

Napapiiri Jeans

- 3 -

STREETHEARTS

- 4 -

Razzmatazz

- 5 -

B-215

1. Ah&Oh Studio / 2. Schwartz & Sons / 3. Hiekka Graphics / 4. Heydays / 5. Super Super

The Breakwall.

- 1 -

Pixie Lott

- 2 -

The Great Anything.

- 3 -

"THE MAD ONES"

- 4 -

BLACK SOIL

- 5 -

1, 3. Paul Tooth / 2. Form® / 4. Cardon Webb / 5. DC

- 1 -

- 2 -

- 3 -

- 4 -

- 5 -

1. Gavin Taylor / 2. Office vs Office / 3. Hiekka Graphics / 4. Felix Lobelius / 5. Super Super

- 1 -

Hobby Tasting

- 2 -

- 3 -

Arca Royale LOUNGE

- 4 -

Soultropia

- 5 -

inprivate™

- 6 -

B·218

1, 4. Bless Ltd / 2. Zion Graphics / 3. Mike Abbink / 5, 6. Studio „The Form"

- 1 -

- 2 -

- 3 -

- 4 -

- 5 -

- 6 -

1. the Beautiful Design, Inc. / 2. Studio Paradise / 3. viction:workshop ltd. / 4. This is Pacifica™ / 5. Zion Graphics / 6. The Official Manufacturing Company

- 1 -

- 2 -

- 3 -

THE GREAT BLANDINI

- 4 -

·ANNO 1950·

- 5 -

the Buccola Group.

- 6 -

1. Ludvig Bruneau Rossow / 2. Jaek el diablo / 3. Jeffrey Docherty / 4. Mike Rigby, Malin Holmstrom, Andrew Droog / 5. Zion Graphics /
6. the Beautiful Design, Inc.

- 1 -

- 2 -

- 3 -

- 4 -

1. Schwartz & Sons / 2. Homework / 3. Olivier Courbet / 4. Giulia Santopadre

- 1 -

- 2 -

1. viction:workshop ltd. / 2. C100 Purple Haze

- 1 -

- 2 -

- 3 -

- 4 -

- 5 -

B·223

1, 5. NNSS / 2. Strømme Throndsen Design / 3. The KDU / 4. RoAndCo Studio

GRAPHIC ICON	INITIALS	STRUCTURAL	IN A ROW	LINE
LOGOTYPE	**TYPE-ORIENTED**	CHINESE CHARACTER	MIXED	CALLIGRAPHY
	MASSIVE	ILLUSTRATIVE	PALETTE	**LETTERING : ORNATE**

- 1 -

- 2 -

- 3 -

- 4 -

- 5 -

- 6 -

- 7 -

- 8 -

- 9 -

1, 2. RoAndCo Studio / 3. Nazario Graziano Studio / 4. Barbara Muriungi / 5. Creative Spark / 6. Ptarmak, Inc. / 7. Bo Lundberg / 8. NNSS / 9. Nubby Twiglet

- 1 -

- 2 -

- 3 -

GREENE & GRAND

- 4 -

EL
TINIEBLO.
— Mezcal 100% Agave —

- 5 -

1. Zion Graphics / 2. Ian Keltie / 3. David Barath Design / 4. Oak / 5. Face.

- 1 -

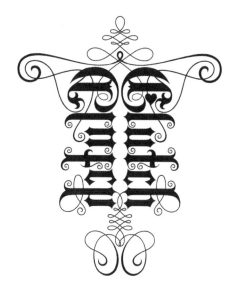

- 3 -

- 2 -

- 4 -

- 5 -

1. NNSS / 2. FUN is OK / 3. Art of Faya / 4. Jaek el diablo / 5. Fontan 2

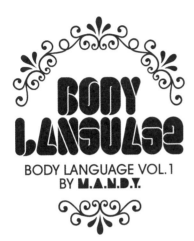

- 1 -

- 2 -

- 3 -

- 4 -

- 5 -

- 6 -

- 7 -

- 8 -

1. C100 Purple Haze / 2. Cardon Webb / 3. A3 Design, LLC / 4. BrfDsgn / 5. Áron Jancsó / 6. Schwartz & Sons / 7. Herburg Weiland / 8. BERG

GRAPHIC ICON	INITIALS	STRUCTURAL		IN A ROW	LINE
LOGOTYPE	**TYPE-ORIENTED**	CHINESE CHARACTER		MIXED	CALLIGRAPHY
	MASSIVE	ILLUSTRATIVE		PALETTE	**LETTERING : STENCILLED**

- 1 -

- 2 -

- 3 -

- 4 -

- 5 -

- 6 -

- 7 -

GRAPHIC ICON	INITIALS	STRUCTURAL
LOGOTYPE	**TYPE-ORIENTED**	CHINESE CHARACTER
	MASSIVE	ILLUSTRATIVE

IN A ROW	LINE
MIXED	CALLIGRAPHY
PALETTE	**LETTERING : STENCILLED**

aliar

- 1 -

AROUND

- 2 -

HEIST

- 3 -

ASSIN

- 4 -

First Point
PROJECT MANAGEMENT

- 5 -

37° EAST

- 6 -

NotJones

- 7 -

CINEMATEK

- 8 -

B·229

1. Mucho / 2. Dimo Trifonov / 3. Manual / 4. Fabio Ongarato Design / 5. Paul Tooth / 6. Ragged Edge Design / 7. NotJones Design /
8. Base Design Brussels

- 1 -

Canterbury
School of
Architecture
UCA

- 2 -

zerooneone·i·
magazine

- 3 -

t h e
MooN

nothing endures
but **change**

- 4 -

Scottish Natural Heritage
All of nature for all of Scotland

- 5 -

1. Face. / 2. Graphical House / 3. TomTor Studio™ / 4. robotalex / 5. Marque Creative

MUSIC IS:
TODAY!
MUSIC IS
MY FUTURE

- 1 -

GRAPHIX.
experimental
typography
and
progressive
illustration
solutions//

- 2 -

TRIANGLE
a project by
ANNA **MOLINARI**
featuring
LEE SWILLINGHAM
issue n. 01
LONDON

- 3 -

GLASGOW
INTERNATIONAL
FESTIVAL OF
VISUAL ART

- 4 -

1. Fontan 2 / 2. George Strouzas / 3. Studio Blanco / 4. Marque Creative

GRAPHIC ICON	INITIALS	STRUCTURAL	VARIATION
LOGOTYPE	TYPE-ORIENTED	CHINESE CHARACTER	**INTERLOCKING**
	MASSIVE	ILLUSTRATIVE	BOLD

- 1 -

- 2 -

M

- 3 -

- 4 -

- 5 -

- 6 -

- 7 -

1, 4, 7. the Beautiful Design, Inc. / 2. AKACORLEONE / 3. cypher13 / 5. Cardon Webb / 6. Alexis Taleb

THE polka pigs

- 1 -

los feliz™

- 2 -

GO VIOLET 日本語

- 3 -

RE OPEN

- 4 -

RAUL BOESEL

- 5 -

DA KINE

- 6 -

NORMAL™

- 7 -

LIVEAREALABS™

- 8 -

B·233

1. Peter Sunna / 2, 7, 8. Negro™ / 3. Gavin Taylor / 4, 6. the Beautiful Design, Inc. / 5. Lucas Rampazzo

- 1 -

- 2 -

- 4 -

- 5 -

- 3 -

- 6 -

1. HelloMe™ / 2. Fontan 2 / 3. Mark Brunswicker / 4. Art of Faya / 5. Negro™ / 6. Super Super

GRAPHIC ICON	INITIALS	STRUCTURAL		VARIATION	
LOGOTYPE	TYPE-ORIENTED	CHINESE CHARACTER		**INTERLOCKING**	
MASSIVE		ILLUSTRATIVE		BOLD	

- 1 -

- 2 -

Rockmonamour

- 3 -

- 4 -

- 5 -

- 6 -

- 7 -

B·235

1, 5, 7. HelloMe™ / 2. the Beautiful Design, Inc. / 3. Negro™ / 4. Grzegorz Sołówinski / 6. Áron Jancsó

GRAPHIC ICON	INITIALS	STRUCTURAL		VARIATION	
LOGOTYPE	TYPE-ORIENTED	CHINESE CHARACTER		**INTERLOCKING**	
	MASSIVE	ILLUSTRATIVE		BOLD	

- 1 -

- 2 -

- 3 -

- 4 -

cyfer electronic dance music internet podcast

- 5 -

1. Annika Kaltenthaler / 2. Fontan 2 / 3. Áron Jancsó / 4. HelloMe™ / 5. Tamer Design & Direction

- 1 -

- 2 -

PORTAS DESIGN

- 3 -

Diversified
Entertainment
Company

- 4 -

- 5 -

Diversified
Entertainment
Company

- 6 -

- 7 -

●Apple Pips
Recordings
Bristol/UK.

- 8 -

- 9 -

B-237

1. Chevychase / 2. Grzegorz Sołowiński / 3. Portas Design / 4, 5, 6. Negro™ / 7. Zip Design Ltd. / 8. Give Up Art / 9. HelloMe™

- 1 -

- 2 -

- 3 -

- 4 -

- 5 -

- 6 -

1, 5. Fontan 2 / 2, 4. Negro™ / 3. Dimaquina, João Simi / 6. Peter Sunna

KAZAK TK

- 1 -

ALVA ®

- 2 -

BAMF

- 3 -

BOMBO ™

- 4 -

boqoc

- 5 -

Uhl

- 6 -

SYSTEM ™

SYSTEM TECHNOLOGY INC.

- 7 -

MAY THE

FORCE

BE WITH ME.

- 8 -

1. Fontan 2 / 2. ALVA® / 3. cypher13 / 4, 7. Negro™ / 5. Dog and Pony / 6. StudioMakgill / 8. André Beato

BioMag
Organic Foods Store
Soon!

- 1 -

- 2 -

- 3 -

- 4 -

1, 3. Fontan 2 / 2. HelloMe™ / 4. Nomad Company

VISUAL GREETINGS
FROM BUSINESS CARDS TO
IDENTITY PACKAGES

- 1 -

- 2 -

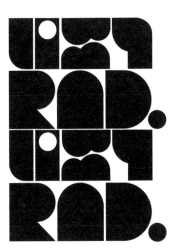

- 3 -

1, 2. viction:workshop ltd. / 3. Cardon Webb

- 1 -

- 2 -

1. Ugur Derinogullu / 2. DRIFTWELL

- 1 -

- 2 -

- 3 -

- 4 -

- 5 -

- 6 -

- 7 -

- 8 -

- 9 -

1. Paul Tooth / 2. David Barath Design / 3. BrfDsgn / 4. The Official Manufacturing Company / 5. RoAndCo Studio / 6. Neubau. / 7. Renato Forster /
8. Hiekka Graphics / 9. Creasence

ART
PRO
CES
S___

- 1 -

- 2 -

THE
MOUNTAIN
COMPANY

- 3 -

–TU
NAN
TES

- 4 -

SPEED
OF
SOUND

- 5 -

MOOD
ÉDITION
09

- 6 -

- 7 -

MINIMAL
DETROIT
TECHNO

- 8 -

PDX
FILM
FEST

- 9 -

B·244

1. Mœ / 2. Negro™ / 3. Ragged Edge Design / 4, 6. Akatre / 5. The KDU / 7, 9. Ian Lynam Design / 8. HelloMe™

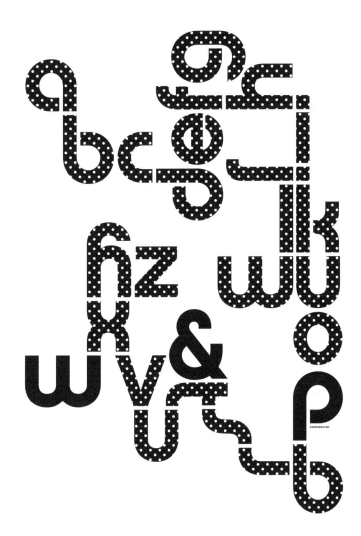

Mark Brunswicker

FROM DREAMS TO REALITY

- 1 -

otto guttfreund foundation

- 2 -

- 3 -

1. THERE / 2. COLMO / 3. HelloMe™

- 1 -

- 2 -

SHHH IFT

- 3 -

Thirty Eight

- 4 -

- 5 -

- 6 -

1, 4. Fontan 2 / 2. David Barath Design / 3. Lee Goater Design / 5. Benjamin Brard / 6. George Strouzas

FLATOIIT

- 1 -

- 2 -

guzmán

- 3 -

CULTURA FALERA

- 4 -

PACO

- 5 -

WWW.KINEMATICRECORDINGS.COM

kinematic
320

- 6 -

APALA 360

- 7 -

ninjas

EDICION NINJAS
BY NEGRO.

- 8 -

1. cypher13 / 2. viction:workshop ltd. / 3. Marnich Associates / 4. Remo Caminada / 5. Lucas Rampazzo / 6. Grzegorz Sołowiński / 7. Blok Design /
8. Negro™

- 1 -

- 2 -

- 3 -

- 4 -

1. BLOW / 2. Resonance Design / 3. Fontan 2 / 4. Good Morning Design

- 1 -

- 2 -

- 3 -

- 4 -

- 5 -

- 6 -

The
Nonlife
ZO.O

没有生命的動物園

- 7 -

1, 2. Taste Inc. / 3. Amazing Angle Design / 4, 5. Nomad Company / 6. Nod Young / 7. biaugust CREATION OFFICE

- 1 -

GILLIAN TOZER

- 2 -

- 3 -

- 4 -

- 5 -

B·252

1. Negro™ / 2. Andrew Woodhead / 3. André Beato / 4. Studio Paradise / 5. Magnus Voll Mathiassen

GRAPHIC ICON	INITIALS	STRUCTURAL	ORGANIC	DIMENSIONAL
LOGOTYPE	TYPE-ORIENTED	CHINESE CHARACTER	LUSH	PHOTOGRAPHIC
MASSIVE		ILLUSTRATIVE	RETRO	

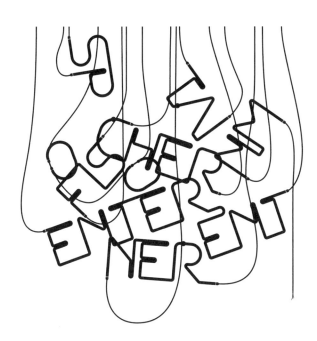

B·253

Homework, Enrico Bonafede

- 1 -

- 2 -

- 3 -

- 4 -

1. Revenge is Sweet / 2, 3. Gaetan Billault / 4. KANIKAPILA DESIGN Inc.

GRAPHIC ICON	INITIALS	STRUCTURAL	**ORGANIC**	DIMENSIONAL
LOGOTYPE	TYPE-ORIENTED	CHINESE CHARACTER	LUSH	PHOTOGRAPHIC
	MASSIVE	**ILLUSTRATIVE**	RETRO	

André Beato

GRAPHIC ICON	INITIALS	STRUCTURAL	**ORGANIC**	DIMENSIONAL
LOGOTYPE	TYPE-ORIENTED	CHINESE CHARACTER	LUSH	PHOTOGRAPHIC
MASSIVE		**ILLUSTRATIVE**	RETRO	

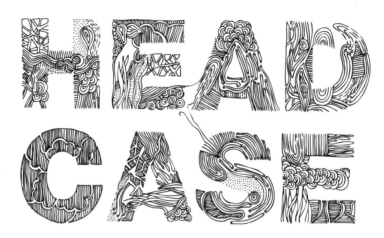

- 1 -

- 2 -

- 3 -

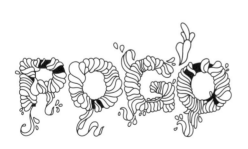

- 4 -

- 5 -

1. Büro North / 2. Thunderdog Studios, Inc. / 3. Cardon Webb / 4, 5. Gaetan Billault

ALVA®

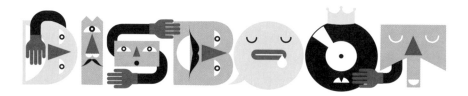

- 1 -

- 2 -

- 3 -

- 4 -

B·258

1, 4. Juntosotravez / 2. ALVA® / 3. VONSUNG

GRAPHIC ICON	INITIALS	STRUCTURAL	**ORGANIC**	DIMENSIONAL
LOGOTYPE	TYPE-ORIENTED	CHINESE CHARACTER	LUSH	PHOTOGRAPHIC
	MASSIVE	**ILLUSTRATIVE**	RETRO	

- 1 -

- 2 -

- 3 -

- 4 -

1, 3. Juntosotravez / 2. Grzegorz Sołowiński / 4. AKACORLEONE

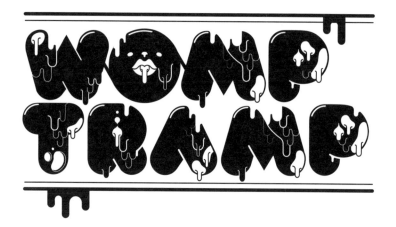

- 1 -

- 2 -

- 3 -

- 4 -

- 5 -

1. Gaetan Billault / 2, 3, 4. Negro™ / 5. HelloMe™

- 1 -

- 2 -

- 3 -

- 4 -

B·261

- 1 -

- 2 -

- 3 -

1. viction:workshop ltd. / 2. the Beautiful Design, Inc. / 3. Face.

- 1 -

- 2 -

1. Gaetan Billault / 2. Giedre Domzaite

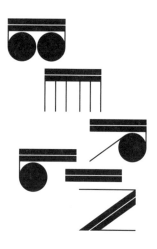

- 1 -

- 2 -

- 3 -

- 4 -

- 5 -

- 6 -

- 7 -

1, 5. Fontan 2 / 2. Konrad Sybilski / 3. HelloMe™ / 4. Negro™ / 6. gardens&co. / 7. Jeffrey Docherty

- 1 -

- 2 -

- 3 -

GLASGOW 2014
XX COMMONWEALTH GAMES

- 4 -

- 5 -

B·265

1. MWM Graphics / 2. ALVA® / 3. Aad / 4. Marque Creative / 5. Homework

- 1 -

- 2 -

- 3 -

- 4 -

- 5 -

- 6 -

1. MWM Graphics / 2. HelloMe™ / 3. StudioMakgill / 4. Homework / 5. TΛKECΛRE / 6. robotalex

- 1 -

- 2 -

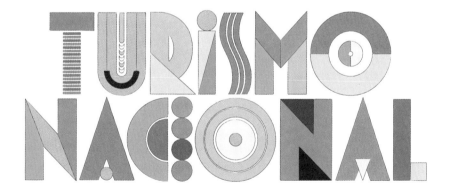

- 3 -

1, 3. Playful / 2. Happy Lovers Town

- 1 -

- 2 -

- 3 -

1. ALVA® / 2. The KDU / 3. Face.

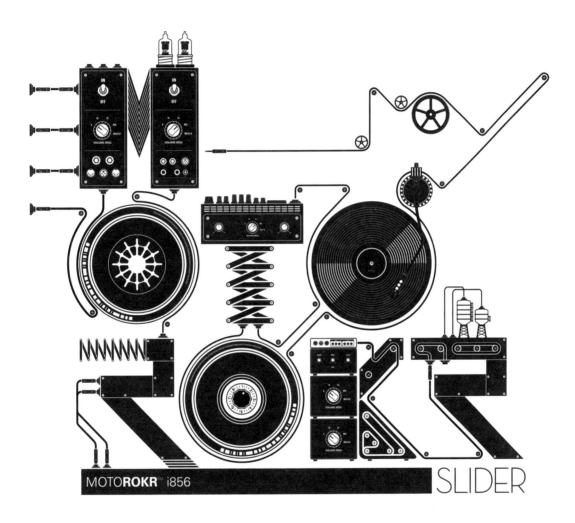

Playful

- 1 -

- 2 -

- 3 -

- 4 -

1. TOYKYO, Kaiser / 2. Studio Volk™ / 3. viction:workshop ltd. / 4. Gee + Chung Design

- 1 -

- 2 -

- 3 -

1. Luke Elliot / 2. Creative Spark / 3. Mikey Burton

- 1 -

- 2 -

- 3 -

- 4 -

- 5 -

- 6 -

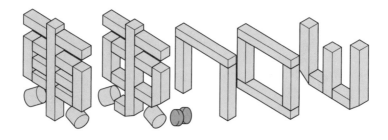

- 7 -

1, 3. Rudd Studio / 2. MWM Graphics / 4. Peter Sunna / 5. Tamer Design & Direction / 6. visualism | design & direction / 7. Ian Lynam Design

- 1 -

- 2 -

- 3 -

1. Peter Sunna / 2. Grzegorz Sołowiński / 3. Kipi Ka Popo

Juntosotravez

- 1 -

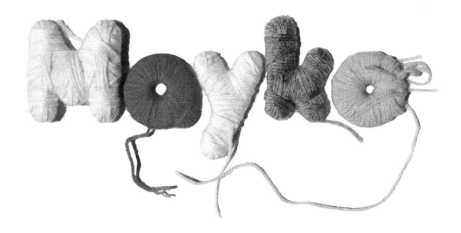

- 2 -

1. unfolded / 2. Pandayoghurt

- 1 -

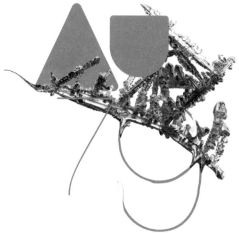

- 2 -

- 3 -

1. Kinetic / 2. Sérgio Alves / 3. Juntosotravez

INDEX

INDEX